FAR FROM THE MADDING CROWD

NOTES

including
- *Life and Background*
- *General Synopsis*
- *List of Characters*
- *Summaries and Commentaries*
- *Hardy's Philosophy and Ideas*
- *Essay Questions*
- *Bibliography*

by
R. E. Jonsson, Ph.D.

Cliffs Notes
INCORPORATED
LINCOLN, NEBRASKA 68501

Editor

Gary Carey, M.A.
University of Colorado

Consulting Editor

James L. Roberts, Ph.D.
Department of English
University of Nebraska

4-20-00   Moonbeam Pub/ 5.00

ISBN 0-8220-0465-8
© Copyright 1973
by
Cliffs Notes, Inc.
All Rights Reserved
Printed in U.S.A.

1999 Printing

Cliffs Notes, Inc.   Lincoln, Nebraska

CONTENTS

Far from the Madding Crowd Notes

LIFE AND BACKGROUND

"It is the office of good literature, the distinction of classical literature, to give form in every age to the age's human mind." Thus critic Lionel Johnson appraised the works of Thomas Hardy, "the English novelist who continues the high tradition of the art, is faithful to the spirit of his age, but faithful also to the spirit of his country." True indeed to his land, Hardy attempted to give form to a small sector of his native southwest England, which he dubbed Wessex. Mindful of changes wrought by nature and the progress of history, and wishing to perpetuate the old customs of his land, he systematically used adjacent sections of Dorset County as the locale for each Wessex novel. These novels are the backbone of Hardy's prose writing.

Thomas Hardy was born on June 2, 1840, in Brockhampton, Dorset, England. At the time of his birth, the old family of le Hardy, as it was once called, was poor and barely above the status of the laboring class. Hardy was the eldest of four children. Too frail for school attendance, he was taught first by his mother, then in the private school of the lady of the manor. At eight, he was strong enough to enter the village school, whose master was competent and beloved. Regular church attendance, family participation in singing and playing musical instruments at church services and village functions, and inveterate walking and reading taught literary, biblical, and local lore to a child sensitive enough to receive and store it.

At sixteen, Hardy was apprenticed to an architect in Dorchester. At twenty-one, he was employed by a prominent ecclesiastical architect in London. His scope as an architect was thereby widened, as were his intellectual horizons. He spent his lunch hours in London's museums. He attended concerts, lectures, and plays, and he continued the study of the classics which he had begun in Dorchester, and also studied French. At this time, too,

Hardy began to write poetry. His first novel, *Desperate Remedies*, was published anonymously in 1871. This and his two succeeding novels, *Under the Greenwood Tree* (1872) and *A Pair of Blue Eyes* (1873), although not popular successes, were favorably reviewed by the critics.

The editor of *Cornhill Magazine* requested that Hardy write a serialized novel. At this point Hardy was harboring the germ of a new idea: he thought of making it a pastoral tale with the title *Far from the Madding Crowd* — and the chief characters would probably be a young woman who farmed, a shepherd, and a sergeant of the cavalry. Loss of another writer's manuscript precipitated the magazine editor's acceptance of Hardy's material merely on the strength of an outline for the first two months of a year's installments. The novel, published in 1874, became Hardy's first popular and financial success.

Success enabled Hardy to discontinue his work as an architect, to marry Emma Lavinia Gifford (in 1874), and to spend the next quarter of a century writing novels. Although there were annual stays of a month or two in London and occasional trips to the Continent, the Hardys spent the major portion of their time in Dorset, called Wessex in his novels. Here Hardy designed and built Max Gate, which remained his home until his death at eighty-seven in January, 1928.

Hardy made many friends in the world of literature and learning, and played an active social role in the London seasons. He wrote assiduously; when he was ill, he dictated his material to his wife. Those of his novels which he placed in the category of "Character and Environment" became best known: *The Return of the Native* (1878), *The Mayor of Casterbridge* (1886), *Tess of the D'Urbervilles* (1891), and *Jude the Obscure* (1896). On the brink of a new literary era, Hardy broached topics and themes with greater frankness and starkness than some Victorian readers liked; consequently, he lived through a period of outraged criticism. Today we wonder at the furor.

Later in his career, Hardy gradually turned again to the poetry he really preferred and, following *Jude*, he worked primarily in this medium. One of his greatest works is the mammoth verse drama *The Dynasts* (1904-8), which is about the Napoleonic wars.

The first Mrs. Hardy died in November, 1912; the couple had no children. Hardy married for a second time in 1914 (at the age of seventy-four). His second wife, Florence Emily Dugdale, had long been a friend of both Hardy and his first wife and had worked as his secretary. After Hardy's death, she published a biography of Hardy which includes his own notes, letters, and comments. Some critics maintain that this biography is essentially an autobiography which Hardy wrote himself.

Hardy was given the Order of Merit in 1910 by King Edward VII. He enjoyed the veneration proffered him, the honors and awards and the visits to Max Gate by the famous. His death in 1928 was an occasion of national mourning. Though Hardy had wished to lie in the family vault at Dorset, the nation wished to honor him with burial in the Poets' Corner of Westminster Abbey. A compromise was effected; as an eminent group of public and literary figures saw Dorset earth sprinkled on the casket of Thomas Hardy in the Abbey, his brother saw the heart of Thomas Hardy interred in the village graveyard at Dorset.

Recognition of Hardy's talents was widespread in his own time and has proved enduring. Translations of his works began right after 1874 with *Far from the Madding Crowd;* there were also early Braille editions. Today the average American bookshop carries more than one edition of Hardy's major works. The motion picture industry, too, has recognized Hardy, and *Far from the Madding Crowd* has been made into a movie.

GENERAL SYNOPSIS

Bathsheba Everdene has the enviable problem of coping with three suitors simultaneously. The first to appear is Gabriel Oak, a farmer as ordinary, stable, and sturdy as his name suggests. Perceiving her beauty, he proposes to her and is promptly rejected. He vows not to ask again.

Oak's flock of sheep is tragically destroyed, and he is obliged to seek employment. Chance has it that in the search he spies a serious fire, hastens to aid in extinguishing it, and manages to obtain employment on the estate. Bathsheba inherits her uncle's farm, and it is she who employs Gabriel as a shepherd. She intends to manage the farm by herself. Her farmhands have reservations about the abilities of this woman, whom they think is a bit vain and capricious.

Indeed, it is caprice which prompts her to send an anonymous valentine to a neighboring landowner, Mr. Boldwood, a middle-aged bachelor. His curiosity and, subsequently, his emotions are seriously aroused, and he becomes Bathsheba's second suitor. She rejects him, too, but he vows to pursue her until she consents to marry him.

The vicissitudes of country life and the emergencies of farming, coupled with Bathsheba's temperament, cause Gabriel to be alternately fired and rehired. He has made himself indispensable. He does his work, gives advice when asked, and usually withholds it when not consulted.

But it is her third suitor, Sergeant Francis Troy, who, with his flattery, insouciance, and scarlet uniform, finally captures the interest of Bathsheba. Troy, who does not believe in promises, and laments with some truth that "women will be the death of me," has wronged a young serving maid. After a misunderstanding about the time and place where they were to be married, he left her. This fickle soldier marries Bathsheba and becomes an arrogant landlord. Months later, Fanny, his abandoned victim, dies in childbirth. Troy is stunned—and so is Bathsheba, when she learns the truth. She feels indirectly responsible for the tragedy and knows that her marriage is over.

Bathsheba is remorseful but somewhat relieved when Troy disappears. His clothes are found on the shore of a bay where there is a strong current. People accept the circumstantial evidence of his death, but Bathsheba knows intuitively that he is alive. Troy does return, over a year later, just as Boldwood, almost mad, is trying to exact Bathsheba's promise that she will marry him six years hence, when the law can declare her legally widowed. Troy interrupts the Christmas party which Boldwood is giving. The infuriated Boldwood shoots him. Troy is buried beside Fanny, his wronged love. Because of his insanity, Boldwood's sentence is eventually commuted to internment at Her Majesty's pleasure.

Gabriel, who has served Bathsheba patiently and loyally all this time, marries her at the story's conclusion. The augury is that, having lived through tragedy together, the pair will now find happiness.

LIST OF CHARACTERS

Bathsheba Everdene

Spirited young mistress of a large farm.

Gabriel Oak

Patient, reliable shepherd; suitor of Bathsheba.

Mr. Boldwood

Gentleman farmer enamored of Bathsheba.

Francis Troy

Lover and, later, husband of Bathsheba.

Fanny Robin

Runaway maid.

Mrs. Hurst

> Bathsheba's aunt.

Liddy Smallbury

> Bathsheba's maid.

Maryann Money

> Bathsheba's charwoman.

Mrs. Coggan

> Employed by Bathsheba.

Cainy Ball

> Young under-shepherd to Gabriel.

Benjy Pennyways

> Bathsheba's ex-bailiff.

Bill Smallbury
Henery Fray } Some of Bathsheba's farmhands.
Jacob Smallbury
Labal Tall

SUMMARIES AND COMMENTARIES

CHAPTER 1

Summary

Twenty-eight-year-old Gabriel Oak was surveying his fields one mild December morning. From behind a hedge, he watched a yellow wagon come down the highway, the wagoner walking beside it. When the wagoner retraced his path to retrieve a lost tailboard, the horses halted. This delay permitted Oak to view the wagon's motley array of household goods, complete with plants and pots. Enthroned atop everything sat a pretty, dark-haired young woman in a crimson jacket. Looking to make sure the wagoner was out of sight, she took out a mirror. Her smile, tentative at first, widened at her satisfying reflection. She flushed as "she simply observed herself as a fair product of Nature in the feminine kind." Hearing the wagoner return, she replaced the glass.

After the two resumed their journey, Gabriel left his "point of espial" and followed them down the road. At the tollgate, the wagon was stopped. Unimpressed by the wagoner's protest that the girl refused to pay an additional twopence, the gatekeeper would not let the wagon pass. Stepping forward, Gabriel handed twopence to the keeper, saying, "Let the young woman pass." The girl glanced carelessly at him. "She might have looked her thanks to Gabriel on a minute scale, but she did not speak them; more probably, she felt none."

Gabriel did not disagree with the gamekeeper's comment on the attractiveness of the retreating girl. But, perhaps irked by her snub, he maintained that she had her faults, the greatest of them being "what it is always. . . . Vanity."

Commentary

"Far from the madding crowd" was how Thomas Hardy wished us to view his beloved native country and the types who inhabited it. Thus isolation furnished both the theme and the title of the novel. *Far from the Madding Crowd* might well entitle his whole series of Wessex novels.

In the first paragraph, the friendly face of Gabriel Oak smiles at us. His features are average, his clothes ordinary, and his "moral color was a kind of pepper-and-salt mixture." Even his idiosyncrasy is a mild one: he wears a large watch with a faulty hour hand. Undismayed, he checks the time by peering into

12

neighbors' windows or by referring to the position of the stars. Unconcerned with time's passing, he leisurely continues to do what he thinks is right. He cares for his fellow beings and is capable of judging them.

Hardy, with the eye of the artist, loved the color and line of the landscape. Thus he personalized nature. His horses were "sensible," his cat "with half-closed eyes" viewed birds "affectionately." His delineation of people was part caricature, as with Gabriel, and part portraiture, as with the young woman whom Hardy shows through Gabriel's eyes. Hardy's first picture of these two young people will be counterbalanced by a well-illuminated, mellowed portrait in the final chapter, when both have matured.

Critics credit Hardy's first profession, that of architecture, with responsibility for his sense of form, both literary and aesthetic. This, his first successful novel, was designed to appear serially; one result of this is the inclusion of a bit of suspense at the close of each installment to keep the reader eager for the next one.

CHAPTER 2

Summary

Swirling winds blew over Norcombe Hill one St. Thomas' Eve. "The trees on the right and the trees on the left wailed or chaunted to each other in the regular antiphonies of a cathedral choir." Mingling with the wintry midnight sounds came the sounds of a flute. They issued from a small, arklike structure on wheels, of the type shepherds dragged about the fields to shelter themselves as they attended to their ewes at lambing time.

Gabriel was keeping vigil. After less than a year "as master and not as man," he now owned (but had not yet paid for) two hundred ewes, which he kept on leased land. With his lantern, he made the rounds of the straw-thatched hurdles around which the ewes stood. Cradling a fragile, newborn lamb, he hastened back to his hut and placed it on some hay before the bit of fire. The hut's furnishings were meager: they consisted of a small stove, a bed of corn sacks, a few medications and ointments, some food, and the flute. Not stopping to adjust the two round ventilating holes, Oak instantly fell asleep on his cornshuck bed. Soon the warmth restored the lamb, which began to bleat. Gabriel roused instantly and carried it back to its mother. The stars told him, his timepiece having failed as usual, that scarcely an hour had passed.

Perceiving a faint light on the horizon, Gabriel went to the edge of the plantation to check. The light came from a hut built into the slope. As he looked through the chinks in the roof, the light illuminated two women tending an ailing cow, and a second cow just delivered of a calf. The older woman was glad the cow was improving; the younger lamented that there was no man to do these heavy chores and that she had lost her hat. All the same, she volunteered to ride to town to fetch cereals in the morning.

As the enshrouding cloak fell from her head, Gabriel discerned the dark tresses and red jacket of the girl he had seen in the wagon.

Commentary

One cannot be unaware of Hardy's sense of the unity of man with nature: the eternal hills of his Wessex, the sounds of wind and weather, the ever-circling constellations, the light at different times of day and different seasons, the growth of vegetation, and the behavior of living creatures. His characters convey a general feeling of being a part of the universe; his narrative captures its rhythms. Far from the madding crowd, he seems to say, man comes into his own. Gabriel is so perfectly attuned to nature that he does his tasks, at whatever hour, faithfully and unquestioningly.

The notes of Gabriel's flute, "a sequence which was to be found nowhere in nature," remind us of Hardy's own participation in a church choir and his playing in an orchestra in his youth; there is an obvious musical dimension to his art appreciation.

Hardy notes that a limited view causes our imagination to fill in the outlines "according to the wants within us." And so it is with Gabriel: "Having for some time known the want of a satisfactory form to fill an increasing void within him, his position moreover affording the widest scope for his fancy, he painted her a beauty." This statement shows us another side of Gabriel He has a romantic as well as a practical sensibility.

CHAPTER 3

Summary

Next morning, Gabriel heard the girl's pony coming up the hill. Guessing that she had come to look for her hat, he hurriedly searched for it and found it in a ditch. Returning to his hut, he watched the girl approach. To avoid low branches, she lay flat on the pony, her face to the sky. No proper Victorian lady would ride thus, but "the tall lank pony seemed used to such doings and ambled along unconcerned. Thus she passed under the level boughs."

On the girl's return to the cattle shed, a farm boy exchanged a milking pail for the bags of cereal she brought. When she emerged from the hut with the pail full of milk, Gabriel approached to return the hat. They exchanged a few civilities which ceased when the girl realized from Gabriel's clumsy speech that he had witnessed her unconventional riding performance. This blunder "was succeeded in the girl by a nettled palpitation, and that by a hot face." Considerately, Gabriel turned away from her blushes. When a slight sound made him turn back, she had gone. Crestfallen, he returned to his work.

Five days later, on a freezing day, the fatigued Gabriel came from his rounds into the hut. Putting extra fuel in his stove, he promised himself that he would adjust the ventilator, but he fe asleep before he did so. When he came to, his wet head was lying in the girl's lap. She explained that his dog, barking frantically, had fetched her from the milking shed and brought her to the hut. Finding no water, she had revived him with the milk. She reprimanded him for his carelessness but smiled when Gabriel tried to express his thanks and told her his name. The girl became a bit coquettish as he tried to shake her hand, but his ineptness and lack of sophistication in not trying to kiss it irked her once again. She left, her name still unknown to him.

Commentary

By having Oak continue to observe from a distance the object of his infatuation, Hardy is able to elaborate upon his description of the girl and her character. Her riding antics furnish a bit of comedy and also warn us that she is not a conventional young Victorian lady. There is a matter-of-factness in the girl's rescue of Oak and in her tart ridicule of his lack of judgment. Her coquettish behavior in the latter part of the chapter contrasts with her earlier hoydenism.

CHAPTER 4

Summary

Gabriel ascertained in town that the young woman was Bathsheba Everdene. "This well-favoured and comely girl soon made appreciable inroads upon the emotional constitution of young Farmer Oak." He waited to watch her each day at the milking and dreaded the time when the cow should go dry and Bathsheba would no longer come to the shed. He constantly repeated her name. "I'll make her my wife, or upon my soul I shall be good for nothing!"

Seeking an excuse to visit her, Gabriel decided to take as a gift a tiny lamb whose mother had died. He groomed himself with care and set forth, accompanied by his faithful dog, George. From behind a hedge near her house he heard a feminine voice calming a frightened cat. He called out that his dog was "as mild as milk," but nobody answered.

Once inside the house, Gabriel told the girl's aunt, Mrs. Hurst, of his desire to marry and inquired whether Bathsheba had suitors. Hoping to make a match, the aunt assured him that Bathsheba had many. Abashed, her would-be wooer replied, "That's unfortunate. . . . I'm only an everyday sort of man, and my only chance was in being the first comer." Forlorn, he walked away but was pursued by the tomboy calls of Bathsheba, who regretted having been away when he visited. Naively, she assured him that there were no other suitors. " 'Really and truly I am glad to hear that!' said Farmer Oak, smiling . . . and blushing with gladness."

Earnestly, Gabriel promised her all manner of things, including a piano. Hesitating over some of the items, Bathsheba said at last, "I've tried hard all the time I've been thinking; for a marriage would be very nice in one sense. People would talk about me and think I had won my battle, and I should feel triumphant, and all that. But a husband—." Finally Bathsheba admitted that she did not love Gabriel, and although the farmer said he would be happy if she just liked him, Bathsheba replied, "You'd get to despise me." Gabriel vehemently asserted, "Never. . . . I shall . . . *keep wanting you* till I die." He asked if he could come calling. She laughingly replied that that would be ridiculous, considering his feelings. " 'Very well,' said Oak firmly. . . . 'Then I'll ask you no more.' "

Commentary

With pronounced humor, Hardy gives the details of Gabriel's courtship of Bathsheba. He spruces up for his visit, polishing the silver chain of his watch and cutting himself a new walking stick. Auntie's boasts of numerous suitors for Bathsheba; Gabriel's offers of a piano, newspaper notices, and cucumber frames; Bathsheba's eagerness to be a bride unencumbered by a husband— these are all amusing and convincing bits of life. The scene also gives us a chance to see more of Bathsheba's vanity and an aspect of Gabriel we had not yet observed—pride.

CHAPTER 5

Summary

"The more emphatic the renunciation, the less absolute its character." This Gabriel learned when he heard that Bathsheba had gone to Weatherbury. Why or for how long she had gone, he did not know. His affection mounted, but he maintained his even temper.

The lambing phase of the sheepfarming over, he returned home for the luxury of sleeping in a real bed. He called the dogs, but only George responded. The younger dog, George's son, completely unlike his sire, was probably still eating a lamb carcass, a rare treat. George was competent and imbued with a sense of his responsibilities. The younger dog still lacked comprehension of what was expected of him.

Gabriel was roused from a sound sleep by the violent ringing of sheep bells. He rushed out, following the sound until he came to a broken rail at the edge of a chalk pit. Young George, evidently inspired by his meal, had zealously chased the sheep, driving them over the brink. Gabriel looked into the deep chasm. There, dead and dying, lay two hundred ewes, all heavy with an equal number of prospective young. There also lay all his hopes for a farm of his own. Gabriel's "first feeling . . . was one of pity for the untimely fate of these gentle ewes and their unborn lambs." Later, without rancor, he did his duty: he destroyed the dog.

Gabriel calculated that selling all his belongings and utensils would just cover the claims of the dealer who had staked him to his first independent venture. The debt was paid, "leaving himself a free man with the clothes he stood up in, and nothing more."

Commentary

Similar to Hardy's use of color to portray external appearance is his philosophy as to the sensitivity of men and animals.

Each creature has a sense of its purpose in life, to a greater or lesser degree. Thus, George's son must be destroyed to prevent further destruction, since he lacks all instinct for his trusted position.

CHAPTER 6

Summary

Casterbridge was holding its February hiring fair. A few hundred hearty workers stood about, each showing the symbol of his trade: carters, a bit of whipcord on their hats; thatchers, straw; shepherds, their crooks. One young fellow's "superiority" was marked enough to lead several ruddy peasants standing by to speak to him inquiringly, as to a farmer, and to use 'Sir' as a finishing word. His answer always was, — 'I am looking for a place myself — a bailiff's.' "

No one seemed to need bailiffs. Toward the end of the day, Gabriel went to have a shepherd's crook fashioned, and he also exchanged his overcoat for a regulation smock. Now, ironically, bailiffs were in demand; yet prospective employers seemed to edge away when Gabriel said he'd lost his farm.

Watching the evening's merriment, Gabriel felt his flute in his pocket. "Here was an opportunity for putting his dearly bought wisdom into practice." His tunes were so well received that soon he had earned enough pence to feel more secure. There was another fair in Shottsford the next day. Hearing that this town lay beyond Weatherbury, Gabriel thought of Bathsheba and resolved to go to the fair via Weatherbury. After going about four miles in that direction, he saw a haywagon without horses beside the road and lay down in it for a rest. After dark he wakened to find the wagon in motion. He eavesdropped on the conversation of the two men in front and conjectured that the vain woman whom they were discussing was Bathsheba. Dismissing the thought, since the woman under discussion seemed to be the owner of a large farm, he slipped out of the wagon unseen.

Suddenly Gabriel saw a fire in the distance. As he ran toward it, he realized that the fire was in a rickyard. His familiarty with the nature of burning hay drove him to hurry to save it before it enveloped the piled-up corn. Others were converging on the fire, too. In the general confusion, Gabriel stood out as one who naturally takes command.

To one side stood two veiled women. They identified Gabriel as a shepherd, for he was wielding a crook, but no one seemed to know him. Finally the fire was extinguished. One of the women sent the other, her maid, to thank Gabriel. The maid told Gabriel that the other woman owned the farm. Gabriel approached her, saying, "Do you happen to want a shepherd, ma'am?" Silently, the astonished Bathsheba lifted her veil. Gabriel mechanically repeated his question.

Commentary

This long chapter abounds with architectural terminology and with evidence of Hardy's skills as an artist and a writer. We view masses of people in motion, but from the immense canvas detailed individual figures emerge as well. Hardy portrays many facets of the fair—speech, customs, costumes, indigenous trades, sergeant, and a recruiter.

Gabriel continues his service as an on-the-spot observer for Hardy. The farmer has been matured by the reverses he has experienced and is learning to compromise. Even as the workers are "waiting on Chance," so is Gabriel. In Hardy's works, many such evidences of belief in fate and fortune exist. Oak's effort to "help" the fates by changing his costume is unavailing. When he decides to continue to Shottsford in his search for employment, the motivation is not too farfetched, for there are not many roads to choose; he is poor and cannot afford an inn. His rest in the wagon and the overheard conversation give Hardy an opportunity to introduce more dialect and to further characterize the Wessex folk.

The animation of the fire scene is a dramatization of country life and of some of the hazards encountered in the seemingly serene landscape.

CHAPTER 7

Summary

"Bathsheba. . . . scarcely knew whether most to be amused at the singularity of the meeting, or to be concerned at its awkwardness." The other firefighters enthusiastically endorsed Gabriel, and so she sent him to her bailiff. All the helpers were to be rewarded with refreshments at Warren's Malthouse. The bailiff, an unfriendly individual, hired Gabriel but could not, or would not, suggest lodgings. He referred Oak to the malthouse where someone might know where he could stay.

As Gabriel plodded along the road, he came upon a young woman standing by a tree. She furnished him with directions to Warren's. But when in turn she asked the way to Buck's Head Gabriel could not tell her. She realized he was a stranger and said awkwardly, "Only a shepherd—and you seem almost a farmer by your ways." She asked that he not tell of meeting her. Gabriel perceived her agitation, saw her shiver with the cold and hesitatingly offered her a shilling, saying, "It is all I have to spare." She accepted it gratefully. He sensed that she was actually trembling. As he went on his way, "he fancied that he had felt himself in the penumbra of a very deep sadness."

Commentary

Hardy is fond of contrasts and antitheses in his phrases and uses these principles in presenting opposing situations and people. Gabriel's generosity and humility are repeatedly contrasted with Bathsheba's selfishness and vanity. Bathsheba's newly aggrandized position is contrasted with Gabriel's recent fall to poverty. The nasty bailiff, "moving past Oak as a Christian edges past an offertory-plate when he does not mean to contribute," is the direct antithesis to the warm and generous Gabriel who gives his last coins to the trembling girl.

CHAPTER 8

Summary

The malthouse was "inwrapped with ivy" and had a cupola on the roof and one window, which formed a small square in the door. Inside, the room glowed with light from the hearth. "The stone-flag floor was worn into a path from the doorway to the kiln, and into undulations everywhere." At one side were a curved settle and a small bedstead. The fragrance of malt filled the room. As Gabriel entered, everyone turned to look at him. An old maltster recognized Gabriel's name; he had known Oak's father and grandfather, and he launched into a garrulous account of them. This made Gabriel seem less of a stranger. He was offered a drink from the "God-forgive-me," a tall, two-handled mug standing among the coals. Gabriel rejected an offer to get him a cleaner cup, and, thus, drinking with the group, he was accepted by them.

There were many country types present, including men of all sorts—the old and decrepit, the scroungers, the cheerful, the shy, and the aggressive. They recalled other drinking bouts and discussed Miss Everdene's family. Her late uncle, who had left her the farm, and her father, a "celebrated bankrupt," fickle and romantic, were properly gone over. Bathsheba had become a beauty, they thought. And her bailiff was dishonest. Gossip was rampant, and all was punctuated by the reminiscences of the ancient maltster.

Gabriel's flute showed from his pocket, and the men asked for a tune. He obliged, confessing that he was down on his luck and the flute had served to earn him a little money. When the men began leaving, Gabriel went off with Jan Coggan, who had offered him a room.

Shortly, a man came running in with the news that Miss Everdene had caught her bailiff stealing and had dismissed him, and that Fanny Robin, the mistress's youngest employee, had disappeared. Bathsheba sent word that she would like to talk with one or two of the men, and those who were left in the malt-house went to see her. On their arrival, she spoke to them from an upper window, instructing them to make inquiries about Fanny the next day in the neighboring villages. Someone reported that Fanny had a soldier friend in Casterbridge.

Gabriel, in a bed at last, lay awake thinking of Bathsheba, delighted to have seen her again. He resolved to fetch his belongings, which consisted mostly of the few books which "constituted his library; and though a limited series, it was one from which he had acquired more sound information by diligent perusal than many a man of opportunities has done from a furlong of laden shelves."

Commentary

The malthouse chapter is important to Hardy's project of depicting his Wessex world. Besides offering some fine sketches of local figures, Hardy presents the atmosphere of the old malthouse, showing us country customs and affording us a general insight into the variety of characters composing this "simple" world. There is a veritable gallery of personality types, all speaking variations of the local dialect, and all charming in their idiosyncrasies. They serve as foils for each other and also as the medium for disseminating background information. Most important, together they function as a collective commentator on country life and current events.

CHAPTER 9

Summary

Bathsheba's home, which "presented itself as a hoary building, of the early stage of Classic Renaissance," was once the manorial hall of a small estate. Ornate stone pilasters, finials, and other Gothic features adorned it. All the outlines were softened by a mossy growth. The entire complex of buildings was mellowed, and its new function, as a farmhouse, seemed to have turned it front to rear, reversing its focus.

Within, the floors, at present uncarpeted, creaked and sagged. Bathsheba and her maid-companion, Liddy, were in one of the upper rooms, sorting the belongings of the former owner. Liddy was the old maltster's great-granddaughter, and "her face was a prominent advertisement of the light-hearted English country girl." Maryann Money could be heard scrubbing, and Mrs. Coggan was busy in the kitchen. A horse tramped up the footpath, and the women were thrown into confusion when they saw that the rider was a gentleman. He knocked, and the responsibility for answering the door was delegated from one to another. Eventually Mrs. Coggan, flour-covered, opened it and announced Mr. Boldwood. Bathsheba could not see him, said Mrs. Coggan, for she was "dusting bottles sir, and is quite a object." Boldwood explained that he was merely inquiring as to whether Fanny had been found.

Later, the girls told Bathsheba that Boldwood was a gentleman farmer, a forty-year-old bachelor. He had befriended Fanny and had sent her to school. Then he had gotten her the position with Bathsheba's uncle. Boldwood, they agreed, was kind, but "never was such a hopeless man for a woman!" He had resisted all female attempts to ensnare him.

Bathsheba, in a petulant mood, told Maryann that she should long since have been married off. The girl agreed: "But what between the poor men I won't have, and the rich men who won't have me, I stand as a pelican in the wilderness!" To Liddy's question, "Did anybody ever want to marry you, miss?" Bathsheba answered, "A man wanted to once." But "he wasn't quite good enough" for her. At this point, a file of employees was seen arriving.

Commentary

To describe the manor house, Hardy draws on the terminology of architecture, with which he is professionally conversant. He adds the mellowed tones of a painter's appreciation and creates the venerable, musty atmosphere of the estate.

This is our first meeting with the gossiping female servants; they are as absorbing as their male counterparts in the previous chapter. Into this preserve comes the very masculine Boldwood. Through conversation with busybody Liddy, Bathsheba learns about him. He is fond of children (he rewards the little gate-keeper), but impervious to womanly charms and wiles.

CHAPTER 10

Summary

After a short wait, Bathsheba granted the men an audience. They had settled on benches at the foot of the hall. Bathsheba opened the time book and the canvas moneybag. Liddy sat beside her "with the air of a privileged person."

Bathsheba announced her dismissal of the bailiff and her intention to manage the farm herself. "The men breathed an audible breath of amazement." Then she called the roster, asking each employee about himself. The men were awkward; some joked, and each seized the opportunity to draw the attention of the crowd for a moment. Young Cainy Ball was made under-shepherd to Gabriel, who spoke to Bathsheba with confidence.

Bathsheba asked for news of Fanny and learned that Boldwood had had the pond dragged, but to no avail. Then Smallbury arrived from Casterbridge, stamping snow from his boots. The soldiers had left the town, and Fanny with them; rumor had it that her friend "was higher in rank than a private." Bathsheba suggested that someone inform Boldwood.

Before dismissing the help, Bathsheba promised, "If you serve me well, so shall I serve you." She would arise early and be watching. "In short, I shall astonish you all."

Commentary

Critics consider this chapter representative of Hardy's work in its character delineation and its humor: Bathsheba is mistress of the situation; Gabriel loses none of his stature, although he is properly humble; Liddy is comical with the sense of her own importance; and the idiosyncratic characteristics of the staff members are developed further. The story has received a push forward.

CHAPTER 11

Summary

Hours later, in snow and darkness, a figure appeared on the public path which was bordered by a river. In the background could be heard the constant gurgling of water. The figure was counting out the windows of a barracks. Stopping at the fifth, it threw a small snowball which "smacked against the wall at a point several yards from its mark. The throw was the idea of a man conjoined with the execution of a woman. No man . . . could possibly have thrown with such utter imbecility as was shown here." After many efforts, the girl finally struck the proper window.

The window opened and a man's voice asked who was there. The girl identified herself as Fanny Robin. She regarded herself as Sergeant Troy's wife because of his frequent promises, and she wished to publish their marriage banns. They agreed to meet the next day. Then she went away, amid the guffaws of Troy's companions.

Commentary

Hardy lets the weather serve to show the interrelation between atmospheric conditions and mood. The approach of winter is well portrayed, and the bleakness of the barracks territory reflects Fanny's dismal situation. The tall "verticality" of the barracks wall is dramatically contrasted with the smallness of the little waif; her credulity is contrasted with Troy's blustering. Using nature to mirror mood or situation is a common device in Hardy. Note the seasons in which major events occur throughout the book. Spring is often a time of happiness and renewal; winter, a time of death and despair.

CHAPTER 12

Summary

Bathsheba followed up her decision to be a good farmer by attending the corn market at Casterbridge the next day. She saw how the men bargained, using facial contortions and gesticulations, manipulating their sticks as props or as prods for livestock as if they were extensions of their hands. She stood out, completely feminine, moving between them "as a chaise among carts." She first approached farmers whom she knew and, as her confidence grew, gathered courage to address others. She had brought her sample bags of corn and was soon pouring grains into her hand with professional skill.

The impression was conveyed that she was learning her business rapidly, despite her femininity. "Strange to say of a woman in full bloom and vigour, she always allowed her interlocutors to finish their statements before rejoining with hers." But she stood firm on her pricings. The men were interested because of her pluck and admired her as much for that as for her appearance.

Only one man seemed aloof—a dignified, striking man of about forty. Because he ignored her, Bathsheba was convinced that he was unmarried. She was intrigued, and on the way home with Liddy she commented on him. Liddy did not know whom she meant. Just then a low carriage passed by with the mystery man in it, and Liddy identified him as Farmer Boldwood, whom Bathsheba had earlier refused to see. He didn't turn in greeting but rode indifferently by. The rest of the girls' trip was spent in conjecture as to the reason for his standoffishness. Had he been jilted? Was it merely that his nature was reserved? For each possibility Bathsheba offered, Liddy parroted agreement.

Commentary

Obviously Hardy attended many country markets, appreciatively noting the mannerisms of the participants. Here he has preserved a bit of Wessexiana just on the verge of change.

Bathsheba's character is developing. Shy in her appearance among so many unknown men, she nonetheless stands her ground for the furtherance of her farm and makes progress in achieving the respect of her competitors.

Though it has been suggested that Hardy is somewhat anti-feminist, the paragraph he devotes to Bathsheba's managerial techniques does not seem grudging. She lets the men talk, but "in arguing on prices she held to her own firmly, as was natural in a dealer, and reduced theirs persistently, as was inevitable in a woman. But there was an elasticity in her firmness which removed it from obstinacy, as there was a *naïveté* in her cheapening which saved it from meanness."

CHAPTER 13

Summary

To while away Sunday afternoon, Bathsheba and the chatter-box Liddy, who, "like a little brook, though shallow was always rippling," practice an old superstition: divining one's future husband by consulting the Bible with a key. Bathsheba turned to the Book of Ruth and, reading, she was a bit abashed. "It was Wisdom in the abstract facing Folly in the concrete." After they went through the ritual with the key and Bible, Liddy asked of whom Bathsheba had been thinking, surmising that her mistress's mind might have been on Boldwood, as her own had been. She was sure that everyone in the church had focused attention on Bathsheba except Boldwood, who sat in the same line of pews. Bathsheba seemed unperturbed by this. As the girls chatted, she recalled having bought a valentine for little Teddy Coggan and proceeded to inscribe it with a verse. Liddy prodded her into sending it to Boldwood instead. Whatever her reason, Bathsheba did address it to the farmer, and from her supply of seals she selected one that said, "Marry me."

"So very idly and unreflectingly was this deed done. Of love as a spectacle Bathsheba had a fair knowledge; but of love subjectively she knew nothing."

Commentary

In four short pages, two giddy girls carry out a silly act which will avalanche into a tragedy. Liddy ("her presence had not so much weight as to tax thought, and yet enough to exercise it") misleads Bathsheba, while her mistress, "bounding from her seat with that total disregard of consistency which can be indulged in towards a dependent," acted on her maid's idle suggestion. Hardy has, in addition, shown us old country customs and, not for the first time, has suggested that women can be guilty of somewhat unpredictable behavior.

CHAPTER 14

Summary

Boldwood sat in his living room, "where the atmosphere was that of a Puritan Sunday lasting all the week." He was increasingly fascinated by the anonymous valentine, which "must have had an origin and a motive." In spite of himself, Boldwood kept reverting to the mystery. He tried to visualize the sender. Sticking the letter in the corner of his mirror, he was conscious of it through the night. He slept badly and rose to watch the sunrise. Unearthly colors played on the glazed fields.

When the mailman came in his cart and proffered him an envelope, "Boldwood seized and opened it, expecting another anonymous one — so greatly are people's ideas of probability a mere sense that precedent will repeat itself." The mailman pointed out that the letter was for the new shepherd, and Boldwood realized that it was intended for Gabriel Oak. Recognizing a distant figure across the field, followed by a dog, Boldwood left to take the letter to Gabriel and to apologize for having opened it.

Commentary

Hardy has furthered the plot by introducing the matter of the anonymous valentine and following it with another letter handed to Boldwood. Additional facets of Boldwood's character are revealed. Boldwood's complexities are here contrasted with Bathsheba's lack of sophistication; her frivolity is set alongside the brooding nature of the farmer. Oblivious to the effect of her whim, Bathsheba has undoubtedly slept the night through.

One is struck by the abundance of figures of speech in this chapter. These are stock in trade for any writer, but they are expertly handled by Hardy. As has been mentioned, Hardy drew his images from many sources — visual, physical, historical, natural, and mythological.

CHAPTER 15

Summary

After a few hours of sleep, the maltster made himself a breakfast of bread and bacon which "was eaten on the plateless system" and flavored with a "mustard plaster." Although he was toothless, his hardened gums functioned efficiently.

Warren's Malthouse served as a sort of clubhouse, an alternative to the inn. Henery appeared, followed by several carters, and expressed the opinion that Bathsheba would not manage the farm successfully. All viewed the prospect of her management negatively. They also disapproved of Bathsheba's new piano and other new furnishings. Henery longed to be bailiff. He felt God had cheated him. A religious discussion followed.

Oak arrived with some newborn lambs to be warmed, for the fields here had no shepherd's hut. When he heard that the men had been discussing Bathsheba, he grew angry and threatened anyone maligning the mistress. The men sought to appease him, flattering him a bit and changing the subject. Joseph now became the victim of taunts directed at his lesser farming skills. Oak admitted that he, too, wished to be bailiff.

Soon Boldwood appeared with Gabriel's letter. It was from Fanny Robin, thanking Gabriel for his help and returning his shilling. She asked again for secrecy and explained that she would be marrying Sergeant Troy. Gabriel showed Boldwood the letter, for he knew that the farmer had been kind to Fanny. Boldwood was doubtful of her marriage plans, for he knew Troy to be unreliable.

Little Cainy broke in, coughing from running, with the news that there were more twin lambs. Gabriel branded the revived ones with Bathsheba's initials. As he left, Boldwood asked Gabriel to identify the handwriting of the mystery valentine. Learning it was Bathsheba's, Boldwood was troubled.

Commentary

In this chapter we see further evidence of Gabriel's steadfastness and loyalty and his unhurried manner of doing what needs to be done. We meet the gossipmongers again. Another link is added to the Fanny Robin matter. Boldwood fears for Fanny and also broods about the reason for Bathsheba's sending the valentine.

Bill Smallbury's remark, "Your lot is your lot, and the Scripture is nothing; for if you do good you don't get rewarded according to your works, but he cheated in some mean way out of your recompense," is a passing comment on what later became one of Hardy's main themes, the indifference of God to man.

CHAPTER 16

Summary

A small congregation at All Saints' Church was startled by the clash of spurs at the close of a weekday service. A cavalry soldier strode into the chapel and spoke to the curate. " 'Tis a wedding!" murmured one of the women, brightening. "Let's wait!"

Through the open door from the vestry they heard the creaking mechanism of the clock indicating half-past eleven. No one appeared, and there was tittering and giggling. So again at the three-quarter hour. "I wonder where the woman is," a voice whispered. This was repeated at the full hour. As the angry sergeant was about to leave, Fanny arrived, breathless, to explain that she had been waiting at All Souls', which she had mistaken for All Saints'. She suggested that they meet again the next day, but Troy refused to go through such a performance a second time. Fanny, trembling, asked when the wedding would be. " 'Ah, when? God knows!' he said, with a light irony, and turning from her, walked rapidly away."

Commentary

Troy is infuriated by his humiliation before the old women and takes out his rage on poor, confused Fanny. Her reaction to his anger is near terror. Though we have seen little of Troy, Fanny's actions do provide some clues to his nature.

CHAPTER 17

Summary

On Saturday at the market, Boldwood saw Bathsheba. "Adam had awakened from his deep sleep, and behold! there was Eve. . . . and for the first time he really looked at her." He found her beautiful, but, unaccustomed to judging women, "he furtively said to a neighbor, 'Is Miss Everdene considered handsome?' " The neighbor assured him that she was. Boldwood was overcome by jealousy as he watched her talking with a young farmer.

Bathsheba was aware of having made an impression and regretted her capriciousness. "She that day nearly formed the intention of begging his pardon. . . . The worst features of this arrangement were that, if he thought she ridiculed him, an apology would increase the offense by being disbelieved; and if he thought she wanted him to woo her, it would read like additional evidence of her forwardness."

Commentary

Hardy briefly shows the new awareness of Bathsheba and Boldwood for each other, and thus gives a new twist to the plot.

We begin to realize that Boldwood is extraordinarily naive about women and probably would be impervious to most pursuit simply because he would not know it for what it was. But Bathsheba's bold "Marry me" is, if nothing else, direct. The frivolity of her gesture is lost on Boldwood, just as the possibility that a careless act might have tragic consequences was lost on Bathsheba.

CHAPTER 18

Summary

Boldwood gave the impression of being aristocratic. He lived in a home recessed from the road, with stables behind it. It was all overgrown with shrubbery. In the stables were fine, healthy horses; all was warmth, contentment, and plenty. Looking after the horses was almost a sacred ritual for Boldwood. "This place was his almonry and cloister in one."

Boldwood's "square-framed perpendicularity showed more fully now than in . . . the markethouse." He paced flatfootedly, his face bent downward. Except for "a few clear and thread-like horizontal lines," his face was smooth. "That stillness, which struck casual observers . . . may have been the perfect balance of enormous antagonistic forces—positives and negatives in fine adjustment. His equilibrium disturbed, he was in extremity at once." Had Bathsheba known the intensity of his nature, she might have been frightened.

It was spring, and one sensed the awakening of the countryside. Bathsheba was across the fields with Oak and Cainy. When Boldwood saw her, his face lit up "as the moon lights up a great tower." He resolved at once to cross the fields to speak to her.

Bathsheba blushed at Boldwood's approach. Gabriel, attuned to her moods, remembered that Boldwood had asked him to identify the handwriting on the valentine, and he suspected that Bathsheba might have been up to something. Finally Boldwood decided not to speak. Bathsheba, aware that she had caused a reaction in the farmer, resolved not to do such a thing again. "But a resolution to avoid an evil is seldom formed till the evil is so far advanced as to make avoidance impossible."

Commentary

Two characteristics of Hardy's writing are emphasized here —the careful sketching of forms, this time of animals, and the sound and olfactory effects as well as the visual ones. Hardy builds up an intensity of feeling. Boldwood is deeply involved with Bathsheba; she recognizes that she has done a foolhardy thing. Gabriel intuitively knows there will be complications.

CHAPTER 19

Summary

When Boldwood finally called on her, Bathsheba was not in. He had forgotten that, being a serious farmer, she might well need to be out-of-doors. Having put her on a pedestal, he found it difficult to see in her an everyday individual like himself. Their relationship was one of "visual familiarity, oral strangeness. The smaller human elements were kept out of sight; the pettinesses that enter so largely into all earthly living and doing were disguised by the accident of lover and loved one not being on visiting terms." Boldwood resolved to find her.

The sheep-washing pool in the blossoming meadow, full of the clearest water, made a pretty spectacle. Several farmhands stood there with Bathsheba, who was in an elegant new riding habit. Two men pushed the sheep into the pool, then Gabriel pushed them under as they swam and, as the heavy wool became saturated, hauled them out with a crutchlike device. Bathsheba bade Boldwood a constrained good-day, momentarily thinking he had come to watch the washing. She withdrew, but he followed her. She sensed his silent emotion. Then, without preamble, he proposed. He stated his age, his background, and declared his need of her.

Very formally, Bathsheba declined. He continued, regretting his inarticulateness, and said he would not have spoken, had he not hope. "You are too dignified for me to suit you sir," she said, and blurted out apologies for thoughtlessly sending the valentine. He insisted, however, that it was not thoughtlessness but instinct which promoted it. Again he entreated, until she begged him to stop, asking for time. "Then she turned away. Boldwood dropped his gaze to the ground, and stood long like a man who did not know where he was. Realities then returned to him like the pain of a wound received in an excitement which eclipses it, and he, too, then went on."

Commentary

Hardy's rendering of the sheep-washing portrays a particularly lovely bit of country life, a seemingly placid performance which contrasts with the intense emotion of Boldwood. In this highly unlikely situation, in the midst of something as earthy as washing sheep, the overwrought gentleman chooses to plead his suit. Bathsheba regrets her "wanton" and "thoughtless" act, is sympathetic toward Boldwood, and is frightened by the unanticipated consequences of her deed.

CHAPTER 20

Summary

Bathsheba, though not in love, nevertheless realized that Boldwood was an eligible bachelor. "He is so disinterested and kind to offer me all that I can desire," she thought. "Yet Farmer Boldwood," the author informs us, "whether by nature kind or the reverse to kind, did not exercise kindness here. The rarest offerings of the purest loves are but a self-indulgence, and no generosity at all." Bathsheba was not eager to be married, nor had the novelty of being a landowner begun to wear off. "Bathsheba's was an impulsive nature under a deliberative aspect. An Elizabeth in brain, and a Mary Stuart in spirit."

Next day, Bathsheba saw Gabriel grinding shears. Cainy Ball was turning the handle of Gabriel's grindstone, but Bathsheba sent him on an errand, offering to sharpen while Gabriel turned the stone. She did not do well, and Gabriel took her hands to show her the proper angle for holding the blades. Meanwhile, she attempted to find out about the men's comments on her meeting with Boldwood. Oak admitted the men had spoken of the prospect of a marriage. When she asked Gabriel to contradict them, he refused to lie for her. He told her that her conduct was unworthy of a thoughtful woman. Bathsheba became sarcastic, saying his attitude might be due to her refusal of him. To this, Gabriel replied that he had long since stopped thinking about the possibility of marrying her. He repeated that it was wrong for her to trifle with Boldwood. Angrily, Bathsheba dismissed Oak as of the end of the week.

Gabriel preferred going at once. " 'Go at once then, in Heaven's name!' said she, her eyes flashing at his, though never meeting them. 'Don't let me ever see your face any more.' " Gabriel agreed. "And he took his shears, and went away from her in placid dignity, as Moses left the presence of Pharaoh."

Commentary

Hardy has interpolated his own views on marriage motives and an intensive psychological study of Bathsheba; the chapter invites careful reading. Bathsheba resents Gabriel's frankness, after having sought it, and even more she resents his statement that he no longer wishes to marry her. The equanimity with which he accepts dismissal enrages her. We know that when Gabriel's helpfulness, on which she has come to rely, is no longer available, she will rue her rashness.

The minute detail with which Hardy draws his characters is exemplified in this passage: "It may have been a peculiarity— at any rate it was a fact—that when Bathsheba was swayed by an emotion of an earthy sort her lower lip trembled; when by a refined emotion, her upper or heavenward one. Her nether lip quivered now."

CHAPTER 21

Summary

   Gabriel had been gone about twenty-four hours when, on Sunday, men came running to Bathsheba to report that many of her sheep had broken into a field of clover. "'And they be getting blasted,' said Henery Fray. . . . 'And will all die as dead as nits, if they bain't got out and cured!' said Tall."

   Bathsheba shouted at the men for not having gone directly to the fields to do something about it. Despite her velvet dress, she too ran to the fields. The animals were very ill. When she asked what to do, the men told her that the sheep had to be pierced to be relieved, and that only Oak knew how to perform this operation. Bathsheba was furious. She thought of Boldwood, but the men told her that some of his animals had been similarly affected by vetch the other day, and he had sent for Gabriel. Still Bathsheba refused to consider this. Suddenly a sheep fell dead, and Bathsheba sent a message ordering Oak to come.

   The men waited until Laban Tall returned with word that Gabriel would not come unless properly asked. After another sheep died, Bathsheba wrote the request and added at the bottom: "Do not desert me, Gabriel!"

   When Gabriel appeared, Bathsheba looked at him with gratitude but reproved him for his unkindness. He went at once to lance the animals. He did forty-nine successful operations. There was only one mishap. Four other sheep had died before his arrival. Fifty-seven sheep were saved.

   "'Gabriel, will you stay on with me?' she said, smiling winningly, and not troubling to bring her lips together again at the end, because there was going to be another smile soon.

   "'I will,' said Gabriel.

   "And she smiled on him again."

Commentary

The chapter serves less to point up Bathsheba's strong-mindedness than as a picture of the vicissitudes of farm life and an appraisal of the constancy of duty on a farm. Gabriel's delay is a matter of discipline, to show Bathsheba that she is dependent on the skills of others and must deal fairly with them.

CHAPTER 22

Summary

"Gabriel lately, for the first time since his prostration by misfortune, had been independent in thought and vigorous in action to a marked extent. . . . But this incurable loitering beside Bathsheba Everdene stole his time ruinously."

On this first of June, Gabriel enjoyed the blossoming countryside and, in the ecclesiastical atmosphere suggested by the architecture of the huge and ancient barn, he participated in the ritual and pageantry of the centuries-old rite of sheep-shearing. Each man played his greater or lesser role in the service. In the background, women gathered the shorn fleeces. Bathsheba made sure that the men would shear closely yet give no wounds. Carelessness was reprimanded.

While Bathsheba watched, chattering constantly, Gabriel sheared a sheep in a surprisingly short time—twenty-three and one-half minutes. Cainy brought the tar pot. The initials B. E. were stamped on the newly shorn skin, and the panting animal leaped away, joining "the shirtless flock outside."

Unexpectedly, Boldwood appeared and talked to Bathsheba as Gabriel continued shearing. The girl left, reappearing in her new riding habit. Distracted, Gabriel cut a sheep. Bathsheba reproved him. Superficially unmoved, Gabriel medicated the wound. The other two went off to view Boldwood's Leicesters.

"That means matrimony," predicted one woman, beginning the gossip. Henery, still resentful that he had not been appointed

bailiff, was most talkative. Gabriel brooded. All the others looked
forward to the feasting which would crown the ritual of the
shearing.

Commentary

Still another fine description of Wessex life is drawn here.
The animation and motion are absorbing as we follow the careful work of the shearers.

Gabriel's tension rises when Boldwood appears. "Gabriel at
this time of his life had outgrown the instinctive dislike which
every Christian boy has for reading the Bible, perusing it now
quite frequently, and he inwardly said, 'I find more bitter than
death the woman whose heart is snares and nets!' This was mere
exclamation—the froth of the storm. He adored Bathsheba just
the same." Note that this quotation follows the indirect refer-
ence in the preceding chapter to a man's using distraction by a
woman as an alibi for not making progress in his profession.

CHAPTER 23

Summary

"For the shearing-supper a long table was placed on the
grass-plot beside the house, the end of the table being thrust
over the sill of the wide parlour window and a foot or two into
the room. Miss Everdene sat inside the window, facing down
the table. She was thus at the head without mingling with the
men."

Bathsheba was sparkling. She invited Gabriel to occupy the
vacant seat at the opposite end of the table, only to ask him to
move again when Boldwood appeared, apologizing for his late-
ness.

After supper, Coggan began singing folksongs. When it was
Poorgrass's turn, he was a bit in his cups and stalled at first. Then
he rendered a composition of his own. Young Coggan became

convulsed with laughter, and his father had to send him off. Tranquility restored, others sang, and "the sun went down in an ochreous mist: but they sat and talked on, and grew as merry as the gods in Homer's heaven."

Suddenly Gabriel noticed that Boldwood was missing from the place of honor. As Liddy brought candles, he saw him within the parlor, sitting close to Bathsheba. The guests asked Bathsheba to sing "The Banks of Allan Water." After a moment's consideration, Bathsheba assented, beckoning to Gabriel "to accompany her on his flute." Boldwood sang the bass "in his customary profound voice." Bathsheba then wished everyone good night.

Boldwood closed the sash and the shutters but remained inside to propose once again. After some hesitation, Bathsheba said, "I have every reason to hope that at the end of the five or six weeks . . . that you say that you are going to be away from home, I shall be able to promise to be your wife." Boldwood withdrew with a serene smile. Bathsheba still had qualms: "To have brought all this about her ears was terrible; but after a while the situation was not without a fearful joy. The facility with which even the most timid women sometimes acquire a relish for the dreadful when that is amalgamated with a little triumph, is marvellous."

Commentary

Hardy offers still another lovely old country custom in his depiction of the farm supper: the crosscurrents of feeling; the power of song, effecting a momentary calm over ruffled spirits; the maintenance of individuality within the group—these are things that Hardy expresses very well.

A verse of the song Bathsheba sings foreshadows future developments in the plot:

> For his bride a soldier sought her,
> And a winning tongue had he
> On the banks of Allan Water
> None was gay as she!

At present, though, it appears that Bathsheba will ultimately accept Boldwood.

CHAPTER 24

Summary

Bathsheba was in the habit of inspecting the homestead before retiring. Almost always, Gabriel preceded her on this tour, "watching her affairs as carefully as any specially appointed officer of surveillance could have done; but this tender devotion was to a great extent unknown to his mistress, and as much as was known was somewhat thanklessly received. Women are never tired of bewailing man's fickleness in love, but they only seem to snub his constancy."

Bathsheba carried a dark lantern, lighting it to peer in corners. She heard the contented munching of animals as she made her return through a pitch-dark fir plantation. Suddenly she heard footsteps and almost immediately stumbled, for her skirt was caught. Recovering her balance, she was aware of the figure of a man seeking to pass her. He asked her to turn on her lantern. The light revealed a scarlet military jacket and also the fact that the soldier's spur had caught the braid trimming of Bathsheba's skirt. His attempts to free her were not very earnest, and finally Bathsheba herself completed the disentanglement.

Gallantly, the handsome soldier, who identified himself as Sergeant Troy, thanked her for the opportunity of seeing how lovely she was. His lavish compliments included the remark, "I wish it had been the knot of knots, which there's no untying!" Flattered and confused, Bathsheba ran to the house, where Liddy told her something of Troy's reputation as a dandy. Bathsheba now regretted having been rude when Troy had probably meant only to be kind. Boldwood suffered by comparison with the sergeant: "It was a fatal omission of Boldwood's that he had never once told her she was beautiful."

Commentary

Hardy has complicated the design in his pastoral tapestry once again. Bathsheba appears to have won a new admirer. In addition to the faithful, stable Gabriel, who has been dismissed as not good enough for her, and the enamored, troubled Boldwood, a man of property who is still under consideration although Bathsheba does not love him, is the charming Sergeant Troy, who has literally—and perhaps symbolically—snared her.

CHAPTER 25

Summary

"Idiosyncrasy and vicissitude had combined to stamp Sergeant Troy as an exceptional being. He was a man to whom memories were an incumbrance, and anticipations a superfluity. Simply feeling, considering, and caring for what was before his eyes, he was vulnerable only in the present. . . . With him the past was yesterday; the future, to-morrow; never, the day after."

Troy was "moderately truthful" to men, but lied to and flattered women. "He had been known to observe casually that in dealing with womankind the only alternative to flattery was cursing and swearing. There was no third method. 'Treat them fairly, and you are a lost man,' he would say."

Bathsheba was relieved by Boldwood's absence. She was surveying the haymaking in her fields when she noticed a red uniform behind a wagon. The sergeant had "come haymaking for pleasure; and nobody could deny that he was doing the mistress of the farm real knight-service by his voluntary contribution of his labour at a busy time." As soon as Bathsheba appeared, Troy put down his fork, gathered his riding crop, and came toward her. Bathsheba blushed and lowered her eyes.

Commentary

Sergeant Troy is an undeniably charming liar who gives no thought to the harm his words may cause. When we remember

Bathsheba's unthinking acts—her treatment of Oak, her valentine to Boldwood—we cannot help but feel some satisfaction that she has finally met her match—and more.

CHAPTER 26

Summary

Troy's first remark was an apology to Bathsheba for his brashness in their first encounter. He had inquired about her identity, he said, and should have known her to be the "Queen of the Corn-Market," as someone had characterized her. He explained his presence now by saying he had always helped in the fields in her uncle's day.

"I suppose I must thank you for that, Sergeant Troy," said Bathsheba indifferently. At Troy's hurt look, she explained that she did not wish to be obligated to him for anything. Undaunted, Troy continued his extravagant praises of Bathsheba's beauty until she admitted her confusion, seeing no basis for his flattery and at first denying that she merited it. But then she began to weaken. "Capitulation—that was the purport of [her] simple reply, guarded as it was—capitulation, unknown to herself. Never did a fragile tailless sentence convey a more perfect meaning. The careless sergeant smiled within himself, and probably too the devil smiled from a loop-hole in Tophet, for the moment was the turning-point of a career. Her tone and mien signified beyond mistake that the seed which was to lift the foundation had taken root in the chink: the remainder was a mere question of time and natural changes."

Sergeant Troy regretted that he could stay only a month, insisting that he had loved Bathsheba the instant he saw her. Disclaiming the possibility of such sudden feeling, she asked the time. Since she had no watch, Troy impulsively sought to bestow his own upon her. It bore the crest and motto of the earls of Severn and had been left to Troy by his natural father. Bewilderment and agitation ient Bathsheba's features an animation and beauty which moved Troy to see the truth in phrases he had used in jest. Suddenly he blurted out: "I did not mean you to accept it at first, for it was my one poor patent of nobility . . . but . . . I wish you would now."

Bathsheba again refused the watch, but Troy did exact her promise that he might continue to work in her fields. In complete consternation, "she retreated homeward, murmuring, 'O, what have I done! What does it mean! I wish I knew how much of it was true!'"

Commentary

This is an excellent study of the glib and suave soldier, proud of his presence, his uniform, and the adventurous elements in his background. Though Troy begins his pursuit of Bathsheba lightheartedly, she is completely taken in by him, revealing herself to be rather gullible and guileless in her confused responses. No doubt her own vanity helps to convince her that he is sincere. Troy, however, seems to have fallen into his own trap, now meaning in earnest what he had said in jest.

CHAPTER 27

Summary

The swarming of the bees was late that June. Bathsheba watched them finally gravitating toward one high branch of an unwieldy tree, forming a huge black mass. Since the farmhands were all haying, she decided to hive the bees alone. Wearing clothes that covered her completely, including gloves, hat, and a veil, she fetched a ladder and mounted it.

Troy appeared and offered his help, declaring how fortunate he was to be arriving at just the right moment. Bathsheba insisted that he don the protective hat, veil, and gloves. "He looked such an extraordinary object in this guise that, flurried as she was, she could not avoid laughing outright. It was the removal of yet another stake from the palisade of cold manners which had kept him off."

Troy brought the filled hive down, a cloud of bees trailing behind it. He remarked that holding the hive made his arm ache more than a week of sword exercises did. When Bathsheba said that she had never seen an exhibition of swordplay, he volunteered to give one for her, privately, that evening. Reconsidering her plan to bring Liddy with her, after Troy reacted to it coldly, Bathsheba agreed to come unaccompanied, "for a very short time."

" 'It will not take five minutes,' said Troy."

Commentary

This chapter contains lighthearted conversation and rare laughter. The ludicrous costuming of Troy adds to the merriment. Also, in this further encounter between Bathsheba and Troy and their plans for still another meeting, the pace of the plot is quickened.

CHAPTER 28

Summary

At eight o'clock that midsummer evening, Bathsheba appeared in the fern hollow amid the soft, green, shoulder-high fronds. She paused, changed her mind, and was halfway home again before she caught sight of a red coat approaching. She considered Troy's disappointment were she not to appear, and she ran back to the hollow. When she reached the verge of a pit in the midst of the ferns, she saw Troy standing at the bottom and looking toward her.

Troy's performance with the sword was precise and filled with bravado. It grew a bit frightening. He pretended the girl was the enemy and brandished his sword about her so realistically that she imagined herself run through. It was a dexterous feat. As a final tour-de-force, he said, "That outer loose lock of hair wants tidying. . . . Wait: I'll do it for you."

"An arc of silver shone on her right side; the sword had descended. The lock dropped to the ground." Next Troy speared a caterpillar which had settled upon Bathsheba's bosom. Only then did Troy admit that the sword was razor-sharp. "You have been within half an inch of being pared alive two hundred and ninety-five times."

Then the man stoped to pick up the lock of Bathsheba's hair. He tucked it inside his coat. Softly he announced that he had to leave. He disappeared, and, overcome by tumultuous emotion, "aflame to the very hollows of her feet," Bathsheba wept, feeling "like one who has sinned a great sin."

"The circumstances had been the gentle dip of Troy's mouth downwards upon her own. He had kissed her."

Commentary

Troy is so completely in command of his sword and so perfectly confident of his skill that he does not hesitate to risk Bathsheba's life for the sake of his performance. His actions have utterly overwhelmed Bathsheba: "She felt powerless to withstand or deny him."

We must not overlook Hardy's own showmanship. He creates a sensuous chapter, with the lush setting, textures, colors, and lighting all playing their parts. He does a masterful job of describing the flashing of lights and the lightning speed of Troy's every move. Hardy was interested in dramatics and here uses his sense of effective staging.

CHAPTER 29

Summary

"Bathsheba loved Troy in the way that only self-reliant women love when they abandon their self-reliance. When a strong woman recklessly throws away her strength she is worse than a weak woman who has never had any strength to throw away. One source of her inadequacy is the novelty of the occasion. She had never had practice in making the best of such a condition. Weakness is doubly weak by being new."

Bathsheba had talked of Boldwood to Liddy, but she spoke to no one of Troy. Gabriel, however, noticed and sorrowed over this new infatuation. He decided to talk with Bathsheba, basing his appeal on her unfairness to Boldwood.

Oak met Bathsheba one evening when she went for a walk. He spoke of bad characters in the neighborhood, wishing to imply that Troy was one of them. He said that in the absence of Boldwood, who would normally protect her, he thought it advisable to take on this role himself. Bathsheba assured him that no wedding with Boldwood was in prospect; she said she had given the farmer no answer.

Gabriel cited Troy's unworthiness. He considered him to be a man without conscience and on a downward course in life. Bathsheba countered his arguments. Oak begged her to be discreet: "Bathsheba, dear mistress, this I beg you to consider—that, both to keep yourself well honoured among the workfolk, and in common generosity to an honourable man who loves you as well as I, you should be more discreet in your bearing towards this soldier."

Again Bathsheba wanted to dismiss Oak for meddling, and again he agreed to go, but only if she were to hire a good bailiff. When she refused to do so, Gabriel refused to leave the farm. Then, "as a woman," she asked him to leave her alone. Gabriel saw her meet Troy but, not wishing to eavesdrop, he left.

Troy had told Bathsheba that he attended church secretly, entering by the side door. Gabriel, doubting Troy's truthfulness, checked this door; he found it overgrown with ivy and therefore impossible to enter.

Commentary

We admire Gabriel for his honesty, fairness, and courage in confronting Bathsheba with her dalliance with Troy. Oak is almost certain that she will not heed him, but he deems it his duty to speak. We understand his point of view when his lack of faith in Troy's veracity is corroborated.

CHAPTER 30

Summary

Despite her promise not to reject Boldwood before his return, Bathsheba could not wait. "The farewell words of Troy, who had accompanied her to her very door, still lingered in her ears. He had bidden her adieu for two days, which were, so he stated, to be spent in Bath visiting some friends. He had also kissed her a second time."

Restless and perturbed, Bathsheba impulsively wrote to Boldwood that she could not marry him. Taking the letter to the kitchen for one of the maids to mail, she overheard the servants gossiping about her latest romance. Furiously insisting that she hated Troy, but with the next breath defending him, she forbade their gossip. Alone with Liddy, Bathsheba confided her love, begging reassurance that all the stories circulating about Troy were not true. Eager to please her mistress, Liddy agreed with all her statements. Bathsheba turned on her: "Mind this, Lydia Smallbury, if you repeat anywhere a single word of what I have said to you inside this closed door, I'll never trust you, or love you, or have you with me a moment longer — not a moment!"

" 'I don't want to repeat anything,' said Liddy, with womanly dignity of a diminutive order; 'but I don't wish to stay with you. And, if you please, I'll go at the end of the harvest, or this week, or to-day . . . I don't see that I deserve to be put upon and stormed at for nothing!' "

Liddy's words led to a tearful reconciliation; she promised always to be Bathsheba's friend, shedding a few more tears "not from any particular necessity, but from an artistic sense of making herself in keeping with the remainder of the picture."

Commentary

Hardy's portrait of feminine frailty and women's weapons is not without humor. Bathsheba does not wish to think ill of Troy, does not want to believe the stories about him, and fights against the possibility of their truth.

Liddy envies her mistress her femininity and her conquests. She is also proud of her position and dignity. Both girls enjoy having a good cry. They agree that "God likes us to be good friends." Liddy assures her mistress that, while Bathsheba is a match for any man, she is not mannish. "O no, not mannish; but so almighty womanish that 'tis getting on that way sometimes. I wish I had half your failing that way. 'Tis a great protection to a poor maid in these illegit'mate days!"

CHAPTER 31

Summary

To avoid Boldwood at his return, Bathsheba planned to visit Liddy, who, granted a week's holiday, was visiting her sister. Bathsheba set out on foot and, after walking about two miles, saw coming toward her the very man she was seeking to evade. Boldwood was obviously disturbed by her letter of rejection and expressed his feeling for Bathsheba in these words: "You know what that feeling is. . . . A thing as strong as death. No dismissal by a hasty letter affects that." He pleaded with her, claiming to be beyond himself, as Bathsheba feared he indeed was. Referring to the valentine, he repeated that she must have had some feeling for him. Bathsheba tried to explain it away by saying, "You overrate my capacity for love."

Boldwood countered that he knew she was not the cold woman she claimed to be. "You have love enough, but it is turned to a new channel. I know where." Bathsheba delayed her reply but could not deny the accusation. Boldwood became unreasonably angry and launched into a long, distraught harangue. "Bathsheba, sweet, lost coquette, pardon me! I've been blaming you, threatening you, behaving like a churl to you, when he's the greatest sinner. He stole your dear heart away with his unfathomable lies! . . . I pray God he may not come into my sight, for I may be tempted beyond myself. . . . yes, keep him away from me."

With that, he slowly went on his way. Bathsheba, unable to comprehend "such astounding wells of fevered feeling in a still man," feared for Troy. Previously she had been in control of herself. "But now there was no reserve. In her distraction, instead of advancing further, she walked up and down, beating the air with her fingers, pressing her brow, and sobbing brokenly to herself." Copper clouds appeared in the sky, presaging inclement weather. Then the stars came out. Bathsheba saw nothing. "Her troubled spirit was far away with Troy."

Commentary

Boldwood, obviously overwrought, has been pushed to the point of potential violence. He bears little resemblance to the remote, dignified gentleman we first encountered at Bathsheba's house. Keep in mind the curse which Boldwood places on Troy: "May he ache, and wish, and curse, and yearn—as I do now!"

CHAPTER 32

Summary

"The village of Weatherbury was quiet as the graveyard in its midst, and the living were lying well-nigh as still as the dead. The church clock struck eleven. The air was so empty of other sounds that the whirr of the clock-work immediately before the strokes was distinct, and so was also the clock of the same at their close." Maryann, alone in the manorhouse, was startled by a stealthy footfall. She saw a gray figure enter the paddock; shortly thereafter, she heard the gig traveling down the road. Thinking that gypsies had stolen the wagon, she ran to Coggan's house, where Gabriel was again staying. The men found that Dainty was the horse which had been stolen. To pursue her, they would need light, quick horses; Gabriel decided to borrow Boldwood's.

They followed the hoofmarks, and were sure because of the shoeing on one foot that it was indeed Dainty. Finally, at a toll-gate, they caught up, only to discover that the "thief" was — Bathsheba!

Bathsheba explained that she had given up the trip to Liddy's for "an important matter." Then, unable to rouse Mary-ann, she had chalked a message on the coach-house door. She said that now that she had removed the stone from Dainty's shoe, she would be able to reach Bath by daylight. The men were sure she was miscalculating the distance, as in truth she was.

"Bathsheba's perturbed mediations by the roadside had ultimately evolved a conclusion that there were only two remedies for the present desperate state of affairs. The first was merely to keep Troy away from Weatherbury till Boldwood's indignation had cooled; the second, to listen to Oak's entreaties, and Boldwood's denunciations, and give up Troy altogether."

Following Troy to Bath insured another meeting with him, but this was something Bathsheba chose not to think about. The rest of her plan was to go from Bath to Yalbury, meet Liddy, and return with her.

Commentary

The deductions made by the men in tracing and identifying the "stolen" horse reveal native skills, as does their estimation of distances. Since both men are sufficiently convinced that Bathsheba's behavior is erratic, Gabriel easily enjoins Coggan to silence.

CHAPTER 33

Summary

After a week, Bathsheba had not returned. Maryann received a note that her mistress was detained. Another week elapsed, and the oat harvest began. As the men worked in the fields they saw a runner. Maryann, who was helping bind sheaves, had an uncomfortable premonition, for she had dropped the door key that morning and it had broken.

The runner proved to be Cainy Ball, on holiday because he had an inflammation on his finger and could not work. The men commented on the advantages of an occasional indisposition which afforded time to get other things done, things more to one's liking. Cainy, choking and coughing, exasperated everyone because he was unable to catch his breath sufficiently to deliver his message. They pounded him and gave him cider to drink. Finally, in spasms, he told of having been to Bath, where he had seen Bathsheba with a soldier. "And I think the sojer was Sergeant Troy. And they sat there together for more than half-an-hour, talking moving things, and she once was crying a'most to death. And when they came out her eyes were shining and she was as white as a lily; and they looked into one another's faces, as far gone friendly as a man and woman can be."

Gabriel, deeply affected, tried to question Cainy further, but the boy had nothing more to tell about Bathsheba, and wanted to talk only about the wonders of Bath. Coggan privately advised Oak, "Don't take on about her, Gabriel. What difference does it make whose sweetheart she is, since she can't be yours?"

" 'That's the very thing I say to myself,' said Gabriel."

Commentary

Realistically, Cainy blurts out the narrative between coughs and sneezes. In his discomfort and obtuseness, he arouses the curiosity of the listeners even more. After a long-winded recital of trivia about the town of Bath, he can offer no further morsel of excitement to climax his tale. The account is not without caricature and humor.

CHAPTER 34

Summary

That same evening at dusk Gabriel was leaning over Coggan's garden-gate, taking an up-and-down survey before retiring to rest." A carriage approached and from within came the voices of two women—Bathsheba and Liddy. "The exquisite relief of finding that she was here again, safe and sound, overpowered all reflection and Oak could only luxuriate in the sense of it. All grave reports were forgotten."

A half-hour later Boldwood walked to Bathsheba's, but Liddy, acting rather strangely, did not admit him. He left at once, feeling that he had not been forgiven. Walking through the village, he saw the carrier's van draw up and Troy's scarlet figure emerge. Troy had once before stayed at the carrier's house. Boldwood, making a sudden decision, hurried home and then quickly returned to meet Troy. As the sergeant came up the hill, Boldwood accosted him, introducing himself and telling Troy that he knew why Fanny had run away. When Troy declared that he was too poor to marry Fanny, Boldwood offered to settle a sum on her. Troy was still reluctant. Boldwood lost his calm and accused Troy of having ruined his chances with Bathsheba. Troy questioned this. Again Boldwood proffered money, assuring Troy that Bathsheba was only toying with him. Troy accepted fifty pounds. Boldwood promised him five hundred more pounds the day he married Fanny. Although Troy said that he thought Fanny too menial for him to marry, he accepted the offer.

Bathsheba approached, not seeing Boldwood, and Troy went to meet her. The astounded Boldwood overheard their loving conversation and Bathsheba's assurance that she had sent the servants away. Troy sent her home, telling her that he would join her as soon as he fetched his carpetbag. Then, arrogantly, he invited Boldwood to accompany him. The devastated farmer lunged at Troy, then realized that he was helpless: Troy was in the bargaining position. Boldwood now pleaded Bathsheba's cause, begging Troy to preserve her honor by marrying her and amazing Troy with the intensity of his infatuation. Troy accepted the remaining twenty-one pounds Boldwood had brought with him. Although Bathsheba was not to know of the financial arrangement, he wished Boldwood to come along to inform her of the marriage plan.

At the door, Troy asked that Boldwood wait outside. After a moment, he thrust a newspaper through the door and held a candle for Boldwood to read of the marriage of Troy and Bath-sheba in Bath. With derisive laughter and a moral lecture on Boldwood's being willing to believe the worst, Troy threw the money out toward the road and locked the door.

"Throughout the whole of that night Boldwood's dark form might have been seen walking about the hills and downs of Weatherbury like an unhappy Shade in the Mournful Fields by Acheron."

Commentary

Hardy does some very deft weaving of the plot threads in this chapter. He has built suspense and now must satisfy curiosity. Bathsheba has made her choice. In the process, the cruel, taunting Troy and the pitiful, baffled Boldwood are contrasted masterfully. We know from the violent reactions (which suggest the influence of the Greek tragedies) that more trouble must follow. Boldwood is so devastated that we know he will not be able to renounce Bathsheba. And Fanny's fate is still unresolved.

CHAPTER 35

Summary

Very early the next morning, Gabriel and Coggan were in the fields. They heard an upper casement window being opened. Troy leaned out. "She has married him!" said Coggan. As Gabriel failed to reply, Coggan, glancing at the averted face, said, "Good heavens above us, Oak, how white your face is; you look like a corpse!" The two men stood near the stile, "Gabriel listlessly staring at the ground. His mind sped into the future, and saw there enacted in years of leisure the scenes of repentance that would ensue from this work of haste." He mused over the reasons for all the mystery. Had Bathsheba somehow been entrapped?

As the men turned toward the house, Troy hailed them. Coggan replied and, after some urging, so did Oak. Troy commented on the gloom of the house, suggesting modernization. Gabriel defended it for its traditions. Troy preferred comfort. After this discussion, Troy suddenly asked Coggan whether there was any insanity in Boldwood's family. Coggan seemed vaguely to remember an old, disturbed uncle. Troy dismissed this information and announced his intention of being out in the fields after a few days. Then he threw them a half-crown so that they might drink to his health. Gabriel was angry, but Coggan caught the coin and urged Gabriel to restrain himself, for he was certain that Troy would buy his discharge from the army and become master of the farm. "Therefore 'tis well to say 'Friend' outwardly, though you say 'Troublehouse' within."

Boldwood appeared, reminding Coggan of Troy's inquiry. "Gabriel, for a minute, rose above his own grief in noticing Boldwood's. . . . The clash of discord between mood and matter here was forced painfully home to the heart; and, as in laughter there are more dreadful phases than in tears, so was there in the steadiness of this agonized man an expression deeper than a cry."

Commentary

Observe how quickly Troy takes over the reins. The reactions of Coggan and Oak are typical: Gabriel needs time for self-control, but Coggan seeks to serve his own interests by serving his new master. The stern pose of Boldwood after his earlier outbursts seems to indicate that he is trying to suppress his true feelings. Hardy's keen observation of many types of people manifests itself in the small but telling gestures, poses, and expressions of all the characters.

CHAPTER 36

Summary

Late August brought storm threats, and Oak worried for the eight exposed hayricks. Troy had designated the evening for the harvest supper and as Gabriel approached the barn, he heard music. The place was decorated with garlands, and fiddlers played for the dancing. The musicians asked Bathsheba to choose a tune. When she said it made no difference, they suggested "The Soldier's Joy." Flattered, Troy led the dance with her. He announced that he had left the army but would remain a soldier in spirit.

Gabriel tried to warn Troy about the hay, but Troy brushed him aside, saying there would be no rain. Besides, this was the wedding feast. Everyone would be served an extra-strong drink, he said. Bathsheba protested that the men had had enough. Troy overruled her and dismissed the women. Furiously, Bathsheba left.

For politeness's sake, Oak stayed a while. As he left, Troy cursed him for refusing a second round of grog. On the way home, Oak accidentally "kicked something which felt and sounded soft, leathery, and distended, like a boxing-glove." It was a toad. "Finding it uninjured, he placed it again among the grass." He knew this to be a warning of foul weather. Indoors, he found another warning: a garden slug had taken refuge in his home. He sat and thought for a while, finally deciding to rely on the instincts of the sheep. He found them "crowded close together. . . . all grouped in such a way that their tails, without a single exception, were toward that half of the horizon from which the storm threatened."

Gabriel, now certain there would be a storm, mentally calculated the potential loss of five wheat ricks and three of barley to be seven hundred and fifty pounds. Returning to the barn to get help to save Bathsheba such a great loss, he saw a peculiar spectacle. The entire male assemblage was sprawled grotesquely in every imaginable position. The central figure was the scarlet-coated sergeant.

Oak realized he would have to work alone. He fetched the key to the granary from Tall's house; rushing back, he found sailcloth and tools. He covered all but two wheat ricks with the cloth, then thatched the barley.

Commentary

Hardy's depiction of the portents of the approaching storm is yet another example of his closeness to nature.

The contrasting pictures of the men before and after the revel are like a pair of companion canvases. Hardy uses his favorite motif of a red-clothed figure at the apex of the composition. In turn, these word paintings contrast with that of the struggling, solitary figure of Oak.

Gabriel cannot be thought of as merely thrifty and practical: "Such was the argument that Oak set outwardly before him. But man, even to himself is a palimpsest, having an ostensible writing, and another beneath the lines. It is possible that there was this golden legend under the utilitarian one: 'I will help to my last effort the woman I have loved so dearly.'"

CHAPTER 37

Summary

A series of flashes and rumblings signaled the closeness of the storm. After the second peal of thunder, a candle was lit in Bathsheba's room. The fourth flash of lightning struck Oak's ricking-rod, and he paused momentarily to improvise a lightning rod. The fifth flash brought Bathsheba into the fields. Once she learned that Troy was asleep, she tried to help stow the sheaves. When a flash frightened her, Gabriel steadied her. Another "dance of death" split trees, and the pair realized they had had a narrow escape. Gabriel told Bathsheba to leave, but she replied, "You are kinder than I deserve! I will stay and help you."

When Gabriel would not explain the absence of the other men, Bathsheba said slowly, "I know it all—all. . . . They are . . . in a drunken sleep, and my husband among them." Bathsheba followed Gabriel to the barn and looked through the chinks: "All was in total darkness, as he had left it, and there still arose, as at the former time, the steady buzz of many snores." As Oak returned to his work, Bathsheba abruptly confessed the reason for her trip to Bath. She had intended to break off with Troy, but jealousy of a possible rival and her own distraction had led her to marry him instead.

The pair continued working in silence until Gabriel sent Bathsheba away because of her fatigue. He worked on, finally "disturbed . . . by a grating noise from the coach-house. It was the vane on the roof turning round, and this change in the wind was the signal for a disastrous rain."

Commentary

This chapter deserves careful reading for its appeal to the senses. The structure, punctuated by flashes of lightning, shows nature in anger, illuminating character, and calling for self-realization and truthfulness.

CHAPTER 38

Summary

"It was now five o'clock, and the dawn was promising to break in hues of drab and ash." The wind grew stronger and uncovered some wheat ricks, and Gabriel weighted them down with fence rails. He continued to cover the barley while the rain beat down heavily. He remembered that eight months earlier he had fought a fire in this same spot, for love of the same woman.

Two hours later, as Oak was wearily finished, wavering figures emerged from the barn. A scarlet one headed for the house. Not one of them remembered the ricks. On his way home, Gabriel met Boldwood, who remarked that Gabriel looked ill and asked the trouble. Oak explained that he had been working on the ricks, and Boldwood admitted having forgotten his. Once such an oversight would have been impossible for him. "Oak was just thinking that whatever he himself might have suffered . . . here was a man who had suffered more."

Boldwood preoccupied with what people thought, said that Bathsheba had not jilted him, that she had never promised him anything. He lamented his fate, his expression wild. Then he roused himself and resumed his reserve, saying, "Well good morning; I can trust you not to mention to others what has passed between us two here."

Commentary

Bathsheba and her three admirers again appear in the same chapter — Troy whistling and carefree; Boldwood suffering from deep emotional tension; and Gabriel remaining loyal to Bathsheba and the land and sympathizing with Boldwood.

CHAPTER 39

Summary

Bathsheba was riding up steep Yalbury Hill in the gig, with Troy walking alongside. He was no longer in uniform. They were discussing his gambling losses, which he blamed on a wet racetrack. Bathsheba tearfully predicted the eventual forfeit of the farm if he continued his present rate of loss. He grumbled displeasure at her "chicken-hearted" wifely ways.

A woman appeared at the brow of the hill and, while Troy's back was to her, asked him whether he knew the closing time of the workhouse gates. Her voice startled him, but he did not turn. When she heard him reply, "she uttered an hysterical cry, and fell down." Troy ordered Bathsheba to leave.

Alone with the woman, Troy asked her why she had not written. She said that she had been afraid to. Troy gave her the little money he had with him, explaining that his wife kept him short. He told the woman to stay at the workhouse, Casterbridge Union-house, until Monday, when he would meet her on Gray's Bridge, give her as much money as he could obtain, and find lodgings for her.

When Troy caught up with Bathsheba, he admitted that he knew the woman, but not her name.

" 'I think you do.'

" 'Think if you will, and be—' The sentence was completed by a smart cut of the whip round Poppet's flank, which caused the animal to start forward at a wild pace. No more was said."

Commentary

We suspect at once that "the woman" is Fanny Robin—in fact, Troy lets the name slip. Otherwise Hardy maintains the term "the woman." Troy's concern for her is real. Fanny is another victim of his inability, or his refusal, to live by anything but impulse. Impulse dictated his marriage to Bathsheba, which now is obviously crumbling. His childish nature is further revealed by his complete disregard for the financial ruin which his gambling losses will eventually bring about.

CHAPTER 40

Summary

The woman continued on her slow way, stopping to rest from time to time and praying for strength. She counted the milestones to encourage herself to proceed. A carriage passing in the darkness lighted her face, "young in the groundwork, old in the finish; the general contours were flexuous and childlike, but the finer lineaments had begun to be sharp and thin." At a lone copsewood she paused. Groping, she selected two Y-shaped sticks and used them as crutches. These helped her to the last milestone, where she swayed, fell, lay for a while, then crawled and fell again.

A dog licked the woman's cheek. "In her reclining position she looked up to him just as . . . she had, when standing, looked up to a man." The animal, as homeless as she, withdrew a step, then returned, sensing her need. Using him as a prop, the woman

slowly moved ahead. They reached a shabby building, so overgrown with ivy that it had become one of the attractions of the
town. The woman managed to pull the bell before falling down.

A man emerged and went for help to get her into the building. The woman revived enough to ask for the dog. " 'I stoned
him away,' said the man. The little procession then moved forward — the man in front bearing the light, two bony women next,
supporting between them the small and supple one. Thus they
entered the house and disappeared."

Commentary

Some critics find this chapter less effective than most — cit-
ing, for example, the interrupting discourse on the manufacturer
of a Swiss prosthetic device which is compared to the woman's
improvisation of a crutch. The agonies of Fanny's journey have
been called melodramatic. Animal lovers protest the use of the
dog, although it seems that Hardy's point was that at times animals have more humanity than people. Hardy's succinct descrip-
tions remain effective, as in the description of the ivy-covered
almshouse to which the force of "Nature, as if offended, lent
a hand."

CHAPTER 41

Summary

Troy asked Bathsheba for money but would not say why he
needed it. Bathsheba commented that his mysterious manner
worried her. Troy responded: "Such strait-waistcoating as you
treat me to is not becoming in you at so early a date." He warned
her not to pry too far. Bathsheba said she felt that their romance
was already at an end. Troy said, "All romances end at marriage."
After more bickering, she gave him twenty pounds from her
household money. He opened the back of his watch, and she saw
a small coil of yellow hair. Troy admitted that it belonged to a
young girl he had once planned to marry.

Bathsheba was jealous, but Troy remained unmoved, saying prophetically, "I can't help how things fall out . . . upon my heart, women will be the death of me!" He left Bathsheba to her chagrin. "She had never taken kindly to the idea of marriage . . . as did the majority of women. . . . In the turmoil of her anxiety for her lover she had agreed to marry him; but the perception that had accompanied her happiest hours . . . was rather that of self-sacrifice than of promotion and honour."

Next morning, Bathsheba rode out to inspect the farm. When she returned for breakfast, she learned that Troy had gone to Casterbridge. She left on another tour of inspection, "finding herself preceded in forethought by Gabriel Oak, for whom she began to entertain the genuine friendship of a sister." She saw him across the fields, and saw also that Boldwood was approaching him. The two men talked earnestly, then called to Poorgrass and spoke with him. Later Poorgrass came toward her and "set down his barrow, and putting upon himself the refined aspect that a conversation with a lady required, spoke. . . . 'You'll never see Fanny Robin no more. . . . because she's dead in the Union.' "

Poorgrass speculated that the cause of death was a general weakness of constitution: "She . . . could stand no hardship, even when I knowed her, and 'a went like a candle-snoff, so 'tis said. . . . Mr. Boldwood is going to send a waggon at three this afternoon to fetch her home here and bury her.'

" 'Indeed I shall not let Mr. Boldwood do any such thing— I shall do it! Fanny was my uncle's servant . . . she belongs to me.' " Bathsheba arranged for a wagon to be filled with evergreens and flowers to cover the coffin.

Later, Bathsheba questioned Liddy about Fanny. Fanny's hair had been golden. Troy had said he knew the soldier who was Fanny's friend "as well as he knew himself." They had served in the same regiment, and "there wasn't a man in the regiment he liked better."

Commentary

This involved chapter has many undercurrents. Along with Bathsheba, we try to ascertain the facts. Boldwood, Oak, and Poorgrass are preoccupied and reluctant to talk with Bathsheba. They evade her questions. Liddy rambles on, suggesting things which Bathsheba is not yet willing to face, and so Bathsheba angrily silences her.

CHAPTER 42

Summary

The workhouse had a small rear door three or four feet from the ground. Here, at about three o'clock, a bright wagon containing flowers drew up. Joseph Poorgrass backed the wagon to the door, and a plain coffin was lifted into it. A man wrote on the coffin with chalk, then covered it with a worn black cloth, and someone handed Joseph a certificate. He placed the flowers over the coffin and drove off. A heavy mist was falling, and gray gloom and quiet enveloped the wagon.

Passing through Roy-Town, Joseph came to Buck's Head Inn, a mile and a half from his destination. With great relief, he stopped at the inn. There, to his delight, were "two copper-coloured discs, in the form of the countenances of Mr. Jan Coggan and Mr. Mark Clark. These owners of the most appreciative throats in the neighborhood, within the pale of respectability," hailed him as he entered. Joseph explained that his peaked look was caused by the load he was driving. They drank, and drank again. Joseph said he had to be at the churchyard at a quarter to five, but the men went on discussing life, death, and theology. Poorgrass grew less concerned with time.

As the clock struck six, Oak arrived. He reproved the men, but, with drunken logic, Coggan explained that all the hurrying in the world couldn't help a dead woman. Joseph was now singing. He denied being drunk but said his malady of a "multiplying eye" had caught up with him. Oak drove the wagon back, reflecting on the rumor that Fanny had run away to follow a soldier. Due to Oak's and Boldwood's tact, Troy had not been identified as the man, and Oak hoped the secret would be kept.

When Gabriel reached Bathsheba's house, it was too late for the burial, and so Bathsheba ordered the coffin brought into the house, for to leave it in the coach-house seemed unfeeling. Troy had not yet returned.

Oak and three other men carried the coffin in, Gabriel lingered on alone, overcome by the irony of it all, and looked again at the writing on the lid. The scrawl said simply, "Fanny Robin and child." He took his handkerchief and carefully rubbed out the last two words, leaving visible only the inscription "Fanny Robin."

Commentary

Even in death it seems that there can be no rest for Fanny. In her coffin, she still travels the roads of Wessex. Appropriately, it is Oak who comes to her aid in death, just as he once did in life; and, finally, her body is given lodging within a house.

Though their behavior seems rather callous, the men at the inn are merely accepting Fanny's death (as they have doubtless accepted many others) as the will of Nature. These people, instinctively close to Nature, accept the results of her actions without question.

CHAPTER 43

Summary

Bathsheba questioned Liddy again about Fanny. Liddy didn't know any more, but said that Maryann had heard tales. Bathsheba refused to believe what Liddy whispered to her, arguing that there was but one name on the coffin.

Feeling that she must draw strength from another to see her through what lay ahead, Bathsheba went to Oak's cottage.

Through the window she watched him close the book he had been reading and realized that he was about to retire. Unable to bring herself to ask him about the matter which troubled her, Bathsheba returned home. Standing near the coffin, she sobbed, "I hope, hope it is not true that there are two of you!" Finally she fetched a screwdriver and opened the coffin. "It was best to know the worst, and I know it now!" The tears came, "tears of a complicated origin." Unable to refrain from hating Fanny, Bathsheba knelt beside the coffin and prayed. When she arose, she was calmer.

The slamming door of the coach-house announced Troy's arrival. He asked what had happened, but Bathsheba would not tell him. The two approached the coffin. A candle illuminated the bodies. Overcome, Troy sank to his knees, then kissed Fanny's face. Bathsheba cried out to him. He pushed her away and told her, "This woman is more to me, dead as she is, than ever you were, or are, or can be." Turning to Fanny, he said, "In the sight of Heaven you are my very, very wife!"

Bathsheba turned and ran from the house.

Commentary

Intuitively, Bathsheba knew the truth and, impelled by guilt feelings caused by the initial surge of hatred and jealousy which she had felt, she showed her pity toward mother and child by placing flowers around their bodies. Troy's emotion and remorse reinforce her realization that her marriage is over.

The title which Hardy gave to this chapter, "Fanny's Revenge," suggests something of the Greek tragedies, as does the dramatic revelation of truth which the chapter contains. But it is not Fanny who is vengeful—it is fate.

CHAPTER 44

Summary

"Bathsheba went along the dark road, neither knowing nor caring about the direction or issue of her flight." Finally she sank down in a brake of ferns. At daybreak, unsure whether or not she had slept, she felt calmer. Eventually Liddy found her, and the two women decided to walk about until Fanny had been taken away. Liddy went back to the house to check, telling those who asked that her mistress was unwell so that people would assume Bathsheba was in her room.

When Liddy returned, Bathsheba lectured her, warning, "You'll find yourself in a fearful situation; but mind this, don't you flinch. Stand your ground, and be cut to pieces. That's what I'm going to do."

They re-entered the rear of the house, Bathsheba withdrawing into an unused attic. Liddy brought in a piece of carpet and laid a fire. From the window Bathsheba viewed the farm and saw the young men at play in the sunset. Suddenly they stopped. Liddy said, "I think 'twas because two men came just then from Casterbridge and began putting up a grand carved tombstone." The young men had gone to see whom the stone was for.

" 'Do you know?' Bathsheba asked.

" 'I don't,' said Liddy."

Commentary

Hardy does not use nature as mere setting: it is an integral part of his story. Bathsheba discovers before her a hollow in which there is a swamp: "The general aspect of the swamp was malignant. From its moist and poisonous coat seemed to be exhaled the essences of evil things in the earth. . . . Bathsheba arose with a tremor at the thought of having passed the night on the brink of so dismal a place." Thus Bathsheba's physical surroundings reflect the dark happenings in her life. She has been brought to the edge of an evil abyss, but she has not fallen into it.

CHAPTER 45

Summary

"When Troy's wife had left the house at the previous midnight his first act was to cover the dead from sight." He then went upstairs to wait for morning.

"Fate had dealt grimly with him through the last four-and-twenty hours." He had taken the twenty pounds from Bathsheba and another seven pounds ten which he was able to muster and had gone to meet Fanny. To his chagrin, she again failed to appear. He waited until the stroke of eleven — "in fact, at that moment she was being robed in her grave-clothes by two attendants at the Union poorhouse." Having watched the bridge and parapet until his patience ran out, Troy called for his gig and went to the racetrack, but he kept his vow not to wager. Leaving town at nine, he regretted not having inquired about Fanny. His return home was a shock.

In the morning he arose, indifferent to Bathsheba's whereabouts. He walked to the vacant grave, then hastened to Casterbridge, where he sought out the stonemason. He asked for the best stone they had for twenty-seven pounds. He paid for it and gave directions for the inscription. In the afternoon he returned and saw the stone placed in the cart which would take it to Weatherbury. Toward dusk he traveled homeward, carrying a heavy basket. In the course of his journey he met the mason's men returning from the graveyard. They assured him that the stone had been set.

At ten, Troy entered the cemetery and found the grave near the rear tower of the Weatherbury church where the land had recently been cleared of rubble to make room for new charity graves. Troy fetched a spade and lantern and read the inscription on the stone. Then he opened the basket and took out several bulbs. He had chosen a variety so that there would be blossoms from early spring until late fall. "Troy, in his prostration at this time, had no perception that in the futility of these romantic doings, dictated by a remorseful reaction from previous indifference, there was any element of absurdity."

Just as he was finishing the planting, he felt rain and his lantern candle sputtered out. He groped his way to the north porch of the church and there fell asleep.

Commentary

Troy's reversal to remorse is interesting. Where he had been callous and heedless, he is now precipitate in his contrition. Gravestone, planting—all must be done at once, and he spends every penny he has on them (although it should be remembered that this was the money he originally intended to give to Fanny). Nor is it surprising to have him remain in the churchyard, intent on completing his service to the departed as soon as he wakes.

CHAPTER 46

Summary

One of the ugly gargoyles of the church parapet jutted out over the area newly assigned for charity graves. This stony land had been uncared for, and as a heavy downpour developed, water gushed forth, falling upon the grave of Fanny Robin some seventy feet below. The carefully planted bulbs were washed away and floated off in the mud.

When he awoke, Troy was stunned into disbelief. "The planting of flowers on Fanny's grave had been perhaps but a species of elusion of the primary grief, and now it was as if his intention had been known and circumvented. Almost for the first time in his life Troy, as he stood by this dismantled grave, wished himself another man." Not informing anyone, left the the village.

Bathsheba remained imprisoned by her own choice. The night before, Liddy had noticed the light of Troy's lantern in the graveyard, and they both had watched it for a time, not knowing whose it was.

In the morning both women commented on the heavy rain and the noise of the water coming from the spouts. Liddy noted that the water used to merely spatter on the stones, but "this was like the boiling of a pot." Asking whether Bathsheba wished to see the gravesite, Liddy also volunteered the information that the master must have gone to Budmouth, for Laban had seen him on that road.

Bathsheba went to Fanny's corner of the churchyard. Here she saw the spattered tomb. Gabriel was standing nearby. He had already seen the inscription: "Erected by Francis Troy in Beloved Memory of Fanny Robin." He looked to see how Bathsheba would react to this. He himself was astonished, but Bathsheba was calm. She asked Gabriel to fill in the hole, and, picking up the plants, she carefully set back those which had been washed out. She requested Gabriel to ask the wardens to redirect the mouth of the gargoyle to a different angle. Before departing, she wiped the tomb clean.

Commentary

Providence is often hostile to man in Hardy's world. Troy wants to change, as his gesture toward Fanny shows, "but to find that Providence, far from helping him into a new course . . . actually jeered his first trembling and critical attempt in that kind, was more than nature could bear."

CHAPTER 47

Summary

"Troy wandered along towards the south. A composite feeling, made up of disgust with the, to him, humdrum tediousness of a farmer's life, gloomy images of her who lay in the churchyard, remorse, and a general averseness to his wife's society, impelled him to seek a home in any place on earth save Weatherbury."

Climbing a hill, he saw the sea. There was a small pool enclosed by the cliffs, and Troy was drawn to it for refreshment. He undressed and swam out between two projecting spires of rock, not knowing of a strong current there. He was carried out to sea and at that moment remembered hearing of danger in this area. He tried to direct his strokes toward shore but failed because of fatigue. Then a ship's boat appeared. Troy's vigor revived, and he hailed it and was rescued. The sailors were part of a brig's crew, coming ashore for sand. They lent him clothes and took him to their vessel.

Commentary

Seeking solitude seems appropriate for Troy at this time. That a boat should appear at the moment when he is drowning is the author's manipulation of the plot, but the action moves so swiftly that the reader is not inclined to pause and meditate on the amount of coincidence Hardy utilizes.

CHAPTER 48

Summary

Bathsheba accepted Troy's absence with a mixture of surprise and relief. Sooner or later he would return, and she feared only the loss of the farm and the poverty which that would bring. To all else she was indifferent: "Perceiving clearly that her mistake had been a fatal one, she accepted her position, and waited coldly for the end."

The next Saturday, when she went to market, a man sought her out to say that Troy had drowned. Bathsheba fainted. Boldwood saw her and caught her as she fell. He questioned the man and learned that a coastguardsman had found Troy's clothes on the shore. Boldwood's eyes flashed excitedly as he carried Bathsheba to the King's Arms Inn, where he arranged for a woman to look after her. He then went out to get further particulars, but none were forthcoming. When he offered to drive Bathsheba home, she declined, preferring to drive herself. Word had already reached the farm, and Liddy met Bathsheba.

A newspaper paragraph told how a physician had driven by the cliff and had seen a swimmer being carried off by the current. He doubted that even a strong swimmer could escape. This and the finding of Troy's clothing seemed to corroborate that Troy was dead. But when Liddy mentioned the need for mourning clothes, Bathsheba declined to wear them. She was convinced that Troy was still alive.

Late at night "Bathsheba took Troy's watch into her hand. . . . She opened the case as he had opened it before her a week ago. There was the little coil of pale hair which had been as the fuse to this great explosion.

" 'He was hers and she was his; they should be gone together,' she said. 'I am nothing to either of them, and why should I keep her hair?' " She held it to the fire but then pulled it back. " 'No—I'll not burn it—I'll keep it in memory of her, poor thing!' she added."

Commentary

Circumstantial evidence satisfies most people that Troy is dead, but something will not permit Bathsheba to accept their conclusions. She appears able to withstand all that has happened and continues to go about her duties, albeit somewhat mechanically. The fact that her sympathy for Fanny outweighs her resentment testifies that she has retained at least some emotional equilibrium.

CHAPTER 49

Summary

Autumn passed and winter came. "Bathsheba, having previously been living in a state of suspended feeling which was not suspense, now lived in a mood of quietude which was not precisely peacefulness." She kept the farm going, however, finally appointing Oak bailiff, a role he had, in fact, been filling anyway. Boldwood lost his crops through neglect; even the pigs rejected his rotted corn. He suggested that Gabriel administer his farm, as well as Bathsheba's, and Bathsheba languidly assented to this plan. "Gabriel's malignant star was assuredly setting fast."

Oak could now be seen "mounted on a strong cob, and daily trotting the length and breadth of about two thousand acres in a cheerful spirit of surveillance . . . the actual mistress of the one-half, and the master of the other, sitting in their respective homes in gloomy and sad seclusion." This led to talk that Oak was "feathering his nest fast." Actually, Bathsheba paid him a fixed wage, but Boldwood gave him a share of the profits. Gossips considered Oak miserly because he continued to live exactly as he had in the past.

Boldwood's devotion to Bathsheba was becoming a madness. Bathsheba's mourning—she had been prevailed upon to wear it—let him hope that there would be a time, however far off, when his waiting would be rewarded. Shortly, Bathsheba paid a two-month visit to an old aunt in Corcombe, and on her return, Boldwood questioned Liddy as to his prospects. She told him that Bathsheba had once spoken of the seven-year period before the legal declaration of Troy's death.

"Poor Boldwood had no more skill in finesse than a battering-ram, and he was uneasy with a sense of having made himself to appear stupid. . . . But he had, after all, lighted upon one fact by way of repayment. . . . though not without its sadness it was pertinent and real. In little more than six years from this time Bathsheba might certainly marry him." Meanwhile, late summer was approaching, bringing on the week of the Greenhill Fair.

Commentary

This transitional chapter serves to show a change in Bathsheba, the reward for Gabriel, and the birth of new hope for Boldwood. Hardy alludes to the biblical story of Jacob serving for Rachel and the importance of the sacred number seven. He was obviously very familiar with the Bible, and his works are liberally sprinkled with such references.

Note that the time has advanced from late autumn to the next summer.

CHAPTER 50

Summary

Greenhill, the summit of a hill with an ancient rampart, was an ideal fair site. There were permanent buildings and also tents. Shepherds who had traveled with their flocks for days thronged in. The colors identifying the owners of the sheep formed a pleasing pattern. A pony wagon for first-aid to the sheep wove in and out. The sheep of Gabriel's two employers were admired for their breeding, beauty, and grooming.

As the day wore on and the sheep were sold, the shepherds turned their attention to a huge tent which would house the Royal Hippodrome's performances. Bands were playing and the crowds were tremendous, with folks like Poorgrass and Coggan adding to the shoving. Two performers' dressing rooms were at the rear of the tent. In one was a young man — Sergeant Troy.

Troy had signed on with the ship which had rescued him and "ultimately worked his passage to the United States, where he made a precarious living . . . as Professor of Gymnastics, Sword Exercise, Fencing, and Pugilism. A few months were sufficient to give him a distaste for this kind of life. . . . There was ever present, too, the idea that he could claim a home and its comforts did he but choose to return to England." He often wondered whether Bathsheba thought him dead.

Back in England now, he was reluctant to return to her; he expected her to be vengeful. He fell in with a traveling circus and became a daring rider. Billed as "Mr. Francis, The Great Cosmopolitan Equestrian and Roughrider," he found himself at Greenhill. Here he played the highwayman in an old love story.

Boldwood asked Bathsheba whether her sheep had done well. All were sold. Save for an appointment with a dealer, she was ready to leave. She inquired whether Boldwood had seen the play "Turpin's Ride to York" and whether the story was authentic. He assured her that it was and politely offered to get her a seat for the performance. This "reserved seat" proved to be on a raised bench covered with red cloth in a conspicuous section of the tent, and Bathsheba was the only person sitting there. She sat self-consciously enthroned, her black skirts draped about her. Peeping from the dressing room, Troy saw her.

Troy explained to the show's manager that he could not go on because a creditor of his was in the audience. The manager, afraid to offend his leading man at this point, made a suggestion. "Go on with the piece and say nothing, doing what you can by a judicious wink now and then. . . . They'll never find out the speeches are omitted." Thus the "creditor" did not recognize him by his voice, and makeup and a beard disguised his appearance.

However, at the next performance Troy suspected that he had been recognized by his wife's former bailiff, Pennyways. Troy resolved to find the man and speak to him. When it was almost dark, he donned a thick beard and wandered about the grounds. Then he spied Bathsheba sitting in the refreshment tent. He found a point outside the tent where he could hear her, and he cut a small hole through the canvas so that he could see her. He saw Pennyways approach Bathsheba, who refused to listen to him. Pennyways then wrote her a note which said that her husband was alive. Impulsively, Troy reached under the edge of the canvas and snatched the note from Bathsheba's hand. Then he ran away. In the confusion, Troy found Pennyways, whispered with him, "and with a mutal glance of concurrence, the two men went into the night together."

Commentary

Hardy terms Greenhill the "Nijni Novgorod" of South Wessex; this refers to a town in Russia once famous for its annual fair.

Hardy's avowed purpose was to preserve all the culture and traditions of his countryside, and he put loving care into the planning of this elaborate chapter. One could argue that it contains too many coincidences, but it must be acknowledged that there are, as well, many colorful and realistic passages.

Troy is still impulsive and shrewd, but he lacks some of his former cockiness. He does not want Bathsheba to see him in his present circumstances. Although surprised at how attractive she still is to him, he wants to discover what he can about her financial situation before deciding whether or not to reveal that he is alive.

CHAPTER 51

Summary

Because Poorgrass had suffered a recurrence of his "multiplying eye," Oak was to drive Bathsheba home. He was still involved in Boldwood's business, however, and so when Boldwood offered to escort Bathsheba, she accepted, still somewhat alarmed by the incident in the tent. Riding beside her, Boldwood renewed his proposal.

He suggested that now there was no longer any reasonable doubt about Troy's death. Bathsheba objected: "From the first I have had a strange unaccountable feeling that he could not have perished." She did not want to remarry, but she did regret her treatment of Boldwood and wished she could make amends. Boldwood immediately asked her to repair the wrong by marrying him in six years, when Troy could legally be declared dead. When he persisted, she asked to delay her answer until Christmas.

Later, Bathsheba told Oak that she was afraid that outright refusal would cause Boldwood to go mad. Oak advised a conditional promise. Suggesting that there was no guarantee that they would all be alive in six years, she deferred to Oak's judgment. "She had spoken frankly, and neither asked nor expected any reply from Gabriel more satisfactory than she had obtained. Yet in . . . her complicated heart there existed at this minute a little pang of disappointment. . . . He might have just hinted at that old love of his. . . . it ruffled our heroine all the afternoon."

Commentary

Boldwood's obsession with Bathsheba is further revealed. Yet, for all the farmer's seeming unbalance, he is shrewd enough to play on Bathsheba's guilt about her treatment of him. This is probably the only effective weapon he has in his struggle to win her.

Oak maintains his surface calm, while Bathsheba, eternally feminine, is piqued when he does not attempt to win her himself.

CHAPTER 52

Summary

The story builds toward a focal point on Christmas Eve. The chapter is divided into seven parts:

1. Boldwood, surprisingly, had planned a Christmas party. Mistletoe, garlands, and decorations were brought in from the woods, and elaborate preparations were made.

2. Bathsheba was agitated and reluctant to go. She admitted to Liddy that she was the cause for the party. To avoid gossip, she would wear her widow's weeds.

3. Boldwood fussed over his newly tailored clothes. When Oak arrived to report on the day's work, Boldwood reminded him that he was expected at the party. "Make yourself merry. I am determined that neither expense nor trouble shall be spared." Gabriel replied that he might be late. He was glad to see Boldwood in better spirits. Boldwood asked whether women keep promises. Oak replied, "If it is not inconvenient to her she may." Boldwood, feverishly cheerful, commented that Oak had become quite cynical lately.

76

4. Troy was in a tavern in Casterbridge with Pennyways, who reminded him that his deceit was punishable by law. He could not answer Troy's question about Bathsheba's relationship with Boldwood. This was to be Bathsheba's first appearance at Boldwood's home. Pennyways still bore her a grudge. He told Troy that Oak was still the boss and that Bathsheba couldn't manage without him.

5. Bathsheba, though plainly dressed, looked very well. Liddy suggested it was because of her excitement. Bathsheba admitted that she was vacillating between feeling buoyant and feeling wretched. When Liddy joked about Boldwood's imminent proposal, Bathsheba gravely silenced her.

6. As Oak helped Boldwood tie his cravat, he urged him to be cautious and not to count on Bathsheba. Boldwood said he knew of Oak's love, and he wished to reward him for his decency. He would increase the extent of his partnership. When Oak had gone, Boldwood pulled out a small box and regarded a handsome ring. Hearing wheels in the distance, he put the box in his pocket and went to greet his guests.

7. While Troy was attiring himself in a high-collared greatcoat and traveling cap, Pennyways counseled against his going to Boldwood's party. Troy argued angrily, "There she is with plenty of money, and a house and farm . . . and here am I still living from hand to mouth—a needy adventurer." In addition, Troy knew he had been seen and recognized in town. Pennyways realized he would have to get back into Bathsheba's good graces in the event of a reconciliation, and so, as a first step, he suggested to Troy, "I sometimes think she likes you yet, and is a good woman at bottom." Troy announced that he would be at Boldwood's before nine.

Commentary

Hardy has kept strict account of the threads running through the novel and here arranges them so that they can be tucked into the complicated tapestry. Structurally, this chapter is carefully outlined in seven sections which indicate what must follow. Troy has a premonition of tragedy, but, characteristically, he shrugs it off and sends for more brandy. Boldwood is keyed up but confident. Bathsheba's feelings vacillate, and Oak is gloomy and apprehensive.

CHAPTER 53

Summary

A group of men congregated outside of Boldwood's house, watching the guests arrive and whispering rumors of Troy's reappearance. They were sure Bathsheba hadn't heard of it but weren't sure whether that was a good or bad omen. They sympathized with their mistress.

Boldwood came out. Not noticing the watchers, he leaned on the gate, murmuring, "I hope to God she'll come, or this night will be nothing but misery to me!" A few minutes later, wheels were heard; Boldwood went to welcome Bathsheba.

Tall, Smallbury, and Samway went to the malthouse. They saw Troy peeping in a window. "The men, after recognizing Troy's features, withdrew across the orchard as quietly as they had come. The air was big with Bathsheba's fortunes to-night: every word everywhere concerned her." The men were unnerved by Troy's return and decided that they should warn Bathsheba. Laban was chosen to tell her but was reluctant; he entered Boldwood's house and left again. He couldn't bring himself to ruin everything. The men decided they had better all join together.

Meanwhile, having stayed an hour and thus satisfied amenities, Bathsheba wished to leave. But before she could go, Boldwood found her and insisted on an answer to his proposal. Finally, she gave her promise: if she were truly a widow, she would not marry anyone, if not Boldwood. The man's restraint broke, and he told her of how he had suffered, of how much he loved her. Sobbing, Bathsheba finally agreed to marry him in six years. Boldwood gave her the ring. Bathsheba said it would be improper for her to wear it. When he persisted, she agreed to wear it just for the evening.

Bathsheba descended from the little parlor to find the party somehow deadened. As one of her men stepped forward to talk to her, there was a knock at the door. Someone wished to speak to Mrs. Troy. Boldwood asked the man in; he was one of the few who did not recognize Troy. Bathsheba sank down at the base of the staircase, staring. Still unaware, Boldwood invited the stranger to have a drink. Troy strode in, turning down his collar and laughing. The truth suddenly dawned on Boldwood.

Troy ordered Bathsheba to leave with him. She hesitated. Boldwood, in a strange voice, told her to go. Troy then pulled her roughly, and she screamed. There was a loud noise. Smoke filled the room.

When Bathsheba had cried out, Boldwood's face had changed. He had taken a gun from the rack and had shot and killed Troy. He then attempted to shoot himself but was prevented by Samway. Boldwood said, "There is another way for me to die." He kissed Bathsheba's hand, "put on his hat, opened the door, and went into the darkness, nobody thinking of preventing him."

Commentary

The action of this chapter is crowded and rapid. One event swiftly follows another, adding to the dramatic quality — as Hardy well knew, having been in his earlier years a playwright.

An atmosphere of inevitability surrounds the climax of the chapter. Once before Boldwood attempted to save Bathsheba from Troy, and when he found he was being tricked he had warned, "I'll punish you yet!" Since that time Boldwood's emotional instability has been made increasingly apparent. His determination to possess Bathsheba is that of a fanatic. Troy has changed little, and he is once again able to thwart Boldwood by trickery and deceit. Never a man of caution, he has ignored a premonition of disaster, and his dramatic gesture costs him his life. We may initially be shocked at Troy's murder, because the chapter has moved so quickly, but we are not really surprised by it once we pause to reflect.

CHAPTER 54

Summary

Boldwood, walking easily and steadily, arrived at the jail. He rang, said something to the porter in a low tone, and entered. "The door was closed behind him, and he walked the world no more."

When Gabriel heard of the catastrophe, he rushed to Boldwood's house, arriving some five minutes after Boldwood's departure. The scene was dreadful. Bathsheba sat on the floor beside the body, Troy's head pillowed in her lap. "With one hand she held her handkerchief to his breast . . . though scarcely a single drop of blood had flowed, and with the other she tightly clasped one of his. The household convulsion had made her herself again. . . . Deeds of endurance which seem ordinary in philosophy are rare in conduct, and Bathsheba was astonishing all . . . for her philosophy was her conduct."

She ordered Gabriel to ride for a surgeon. In town, Gabriel also stopped to notify the authorities and so learned of Boldwood's surrender. Meanwhile, Bathsheba had Troy moved home. Liddy admitted the doctor, telling him that Bathsheba had locked herself in the room with the body. She had left orders that the surgeon and Parson Thirdly were to be admitted.

The surgeon found Troy's body lit by candles and draped in white. Returning to Oak and the parson, the doctor remarked in a subdued voice, "It is all done. . . . this mere girl! She must have the nerve of a stoic!"

"The heart of a wife, merely," Bathsheba whispered behind him. Then, silently, she sank to the floor. She had a series of fainting fits that for a time seemed serious, but the surgeon attended her. Liddy was told to watch over her during the night. She heard her mistress moan, "O it is my fault—how can I live!"

Commentary

Bathsheba's display of strength reminds the surgeon of the ancient stoics; it is also reminiscent of the great women of Greek tragedy. Then, having done what was required of her, Bathsheba can yield to weakness (and Victorian tradition) and faint away. This was a common frailty in the women of Victorian times, both in literature and in life. Bathsheba's stern conscience, which continues to trouble her, is another typical Victorian characteristic.

CHAPTER 55

Summary

On a bleak day three months later, a number of people gathered on Yalbury Hill. The high sheriff waited in a carriage. Another carriage arrived carrying the judge of the circuit court; he switched carriages, trumpets flourished, and a procession went into town. Bathsheba's men discussed their hopes that the judge would be merciful to Boldwood.

Much had been learned of Boldwood's behavior. No one had guessed the extent of his derangement. The closets in his home were found to contain an expensive and elegant collection of ladies' clothes, muffs, and jewelry, all wrapped, labeled "Bathsheba Boldwood," and dated six years ahead. Boldwood had bought the things in Bath and elsewhere and had brought them to his home.

The group which gathered at the malthouse thoroughly discussed the question of Boldwood's odd behavior. Once the suggestion had been raised, it was simple to find examples of the farmer's oddity. "The conviction that Boldwood had not been morally responsible for his later acts now became general." But Gabriel arrived to announce the verdict: "Boldwood, as every one supposed he would do, had pleaded guilty, and had been sentenced to death."

A petition was sent to the home secretary, asking for reconsideration of the verdict because of Boldwood's state of mind. But not too many inhabitants of Casterbridge signed it. Shopkeepers resented Boldwood's patronage of other towns to purchase the finery for Bathsheba. A few merciful men prodded others into signing.

The reply to the petition had not arrived by the Friday preceding the day set for the execution. Coming from the jail where he had bidden farewell to Boldwood, Gabriel saw the scaffold being erected. Bathsheba was in bed, wasting away. She constantly asked whether the messenger had arrived with an answer to the petition. Gabriel too was worried. His "anxiety was great that Boldwood might be saved, even though in his conscience he felt that he ought to die; for there had been qualities in the farmer which Oak loved."

At last, late that night, a rider brought the answer they awaited. The sentence had been commuted to "confinement during Her Majesty's pleasure."

" 'Hurrah!' said Coggan, with a swelling heart. 'God's above the devil yet!' "

Commentary

In this chapter we learn most of the news through hearsay and the expression of the views of the townsfolk. Liddy, for example, tells us that Bathsheba's "sufferings have been dreadful," and that she fears for her mistress' sanity if Boldwood is executed. Oak, as always, remains steadfast.

CHAPTER 56

Summary

   "Bathsheba revived with the spring. The utter prostration that had followed the low fever from which she had suffered diminished perceptibly when all uncertainty upon every subject had come to an end." In summer, she eventually attempted to walk to town. She passed the church and heard the choir practicing. Then she stood before Fanny Robin's grave and read the words which Troy had had inscribed. Beneath them was a new inscription: "In the same Grave lie The Remains of the aforesaid Francis Troy. . . ."

   The children in the church were rehearsing a hymn, "Lead, Kindly Light." Bathsheba, recalling all that had happened, wept. Oak approached. He had been inside the church, singing with the choir.

   Their talk was formal, Bathsheba addressing him as Mr. Oak. As they walked back, Gabriel spoke of his plans to leave England and go to California. He admitted that he had an option to buy Boldwood's farm, but he had decided merely to finish out his year as manager. Bathsheba was upset that Gabriel, whom she now considered an old friend, would no longer be there to help her. Gabriel answered that her very helplessness was another reason for his planned departure. From that day on, he avoided Bathsheba.

   Fall and winter passed, and when Bathsheba finally received the long-expected letter of resignation from Oak, she wept bitterly. Then she donned her bonnet and went to his house. He did not realize it was she at first—then, apologetically, he admitted her. His bachelor quarters had no comforts, he said, for ladies.

   Bathsheba asked if she had offended him. Gabriel explained that, on the contrary, he was leaving because there was gossip that he was waiting to buy Boldwood's farm just so that he would be rich enough to court Bathsheba.

"Bathsheba did not look quite so alarmed as if a cannon had been discharged by her ear, which was what Oak had expected. 'Marrying me! I didn't know it was that you meant. . . . Such a thing as that is too absurd—too soon—to think of, by far!'" Gabriel heard only the "absurd," not the "too soon," and their talk continued at cross purposes until Gabriel said that he wished he knew if she would let him court her. Bathsheba tearfully assured him that he would never know whether she would have him unless he asked. The two found release in laughter, finally throwing off the inhibitions and constraints of employer and employee. To Bathsheba's embarrassed remark that she had come courting him, Gabriel replied that it was his due for having long danced to her tune.

"They spoke very little of their mutual feeling; pretty phrases and warm expressions being probably unnecessary between such tried friends. . . . when the two who are thrown together begin first by knowing the rougher sides of each other's character, and not the best till further on."

Commentary

Hardy is now winding up the plot details swiftly and directly. It is in character that Bathsheba's first visit is to the churchyard, and that Gabriel's life is neatly ordered. Somewhat aloof since the tragedy, Gabriel no longer overtly aspires to win Bathsheba, but he does resign to protect her reputation. Hardy spares us a coy or saccharine close, ending rather with a bit of wise philosophy about the basis of a sound marriage.

CHAPTER 57

Summary

" 'The most private, secret, plainest wedding that it is possible to have.' Those had been Bathsheba's words to Oak one evening, some time after the events of the preceding chapter, and he meditated a full hour by the clock upon how to carry out her wishes to the letter."

There was the matter of the license. Oak met Coggan in town and admitted his plans but swore his friend to secrecy. Coggan delivered a message to the parish clerk, Laban Tall, telling him to meet the mistress next morning and to be wearing his best clothes. He told the clerk's curious wife, "Mind, het or wet, blow or snow, he must come. . . . 'Tis very particular indeed. The fact is, 'tis to witness her sign some law-work about taking shares wi' another farmer for a long span o' years. There, that's what 'tis, and now I've told 'ee, Mother Tall, in a way I shouldn't ha' done if I hadn't loved 'ee so hopelessly well." The next call at the vicar's excited no curiosity.

Bathsheba awakened before Liddy's call. As Liddy was brushing her mistress' hair, Bathsheba told the inquisitive girl that Oak was coming to dinner. Liddy guessed the purport and was excited.

Oak arrived with an umbrella, and, a short time later, swathed head to foot in greatcoats, he and Bathsheba, each under an umbrella, walked into town, like sensible people who were on a brief errand. In the church were Tall, Liddy, and the parson.

After the wedding, there was tea at Bathsheba's. Oak had decided to move in, since he did not as yet have appropriate furnishings in his house. "Just as Bathsheba was pouring out a cup of tea, their ears were greeted by the firing of a cannon, followed by what seemed like a tremendous blowing of trumpets in the front of the house. . . . Oak took up the light and went into the porch, followed by Bathsheba with a shawl over her head." A group of male figures set up a loud hurrah; there was another cannon shot, followed by a "hideous clang of music" from assorted ancient and venerable instruments. Oak said a warm, "Come in, souls, and have something to eat and drink wi' me and my wife." "Not to-night," was the unselfish reply. The men suggested that drinks be sent to Warren's, instead. Oak gladly accepted the suggestion.

Commenting on the ease with which Oak said "my wife," the friends withdrew, Oak laughing and Bathsheba smiling. As they moved away, Poorgrass had the last word: "And I wish him joy o' her. . . . since 'tis as 'tis, why, it might have been worse, and I feel my thanks accordingly."

Commentary

The simple close is both appropriate and artistic. We feel that this time things will be all right. Oak's manner contrasts with Troy's after his marriage, when he was so condescending toward the hired help. Though Oak and Bathsheba are the focal point, the scene is mellowed and subdued. There is a voluntary outgoing of affection toward the couple and a friendly understanding of the roles they all will play.

HARDY'S PHILOSOPHY AND IDEAS

Hardy is primarily a storyteller and should be viewed more as a chronicler of moods and deeds than as a philosopher. Yet a novel such as *Far from the Madding Crowd*, which raises many questions about society, religion, morals, and the contrast between a good life and its rewards, is bound to make the reader curious about the author who brings them up.

Hardy lived in an age of transition. The industrial revolution was in the process of destroying the agricultural life, and the subsequent shifting of population caused a disintegration of rural customs and traditions which had meant security, stability, and dignity for the people. It was a period when fundamental beliefs —religious, social, scientific, and political—were shaken to their core and brought in their stead the "ache of modernism." The new philosophies failed to satisfy the emotional needs of many people. As a young man, Hardy read Darwin's *Origin of the Species* and *Essays and Reviews* (the manifesto of a few churchmen who held radical theological opinions), both of which were to influence his views toward religion. He found it difficult, if not impossible, to reconcile the idea of a beneficent, omnipotent, and omniscient diety with the fact of omnipresent evil and the persistent tendency of circumstances toward unhappiness.

When one thinks of Hardy the novelist, that aspect of his work which comes to mind most readily is his frequent use of chance and circumstances in the development of his plots. But the reader must learn to view Hardy's stories in the light of the author's fatalistic outlook on life, for Hardy fluctuates between fatalism and determinism. Fatalism is a view of life which acknowledges that all action is controlled by the nature of things, or by a Fate which is a great, impersonal, primitive force existing through all eternity, absolutely independent of human wills and superior to any god created by man. Determinism, on the other hand, acknowledges that man's struggle against the will behind things is of no avail, that the laws of cause and effect are in operation—that is, the human will is not free and human beings have no control over their own destiny, try as they may. Hardy sees life in terms of action, in the doomed struggle against the circumstantial forces against happiness. Incident, for example, plays an important role in causing joy or pain, and often an act of indiscretion in early youth can wreck one's chances for happiness. In Hardy's novels, then, Fate appears as an artistic motif in a great variety of forms—chance and coincidence, nature, time, woman, and convention. None is Fate itself, but rather all of these are manifestations of the Immanent Will.

The use of chance and coincidence as a means of furthering the plot was a technique used by many Victorian authors but with Hardy it becomes something more than a mere device. Fateful incidents (overheard conversations and undelivered letters, for instance) are the forces working against mere man in his efforts to control his own destiny. In addition, Fate appears in the form of nature, endowing it with varying moods which affect the lives of the characters. Those who are most in harmony with their environment are usually the most contented; similarly, those who can appreciate the joys of nature can find solace in it. Yet nature can take on sinister aspects, becoming more of an actor than just a setting for the action.

Besides the importance of nature in Hardy's novels, one should consider the concept of time. There is tremendous importance placed on the moment, for time is a great series of moments. The joys of life are transitory and the moments of joy may be turned to bitterness by time. Woman, also, is used by Hardy as one of Fate's most potent instruments for opposing man's happiness. Closer to primitive feelings than man, woman is helpless in the hands of Fate and carries out Fate's work. In her search for love, the motivating passion of her life, woman becomes an agent in her own destiny. In short, one is, according to Hardy, powerless to change the workings of Fate, but those things which are contrived by man — social laws and convention, for example — and which work against him can be changed by man. Man is not hopelessly doomed.

ESSAY QUESTIONS

1. Show how Hardy indicated the passage of time, rarely using actual dates.

2. Discuss how the changing seasons are bound up with the story.

3. Discuss Hardy's use of biblical, literary, and artistic allusions.

4. Show in what ways Bathsheba's character changes and in what ways it remains the same.

5. Show how Victorian ideas of morality affect the lives of Fanny Robin; Sergeant Troy; Bathsheba.

BIBLIOGRAPHY

ABERCROMBIE, LASCELLES. *Thomas Hardy.* London: Martin Secker, 1912.

ALLEN, WALTER. *The English Novel.* New York: E. P. Dutton, 1954.

BLUNDEN, EDMUND. *Thomas Hardy.* New York: Macmillan, 1962.

BROWN, DOUGLAS. *Thomas Hardy*. London: Longmans, Green, 1954.

CECIL, DAVID. *Victorian Novelists*. Chicago: University of Chicago Press, 1958.

CHEW, SAMUEL C. *Thomas Hardy, Poet and Novelist*. New York: Russell & Russell, 1964.

Colby College Library. *A Century of Thomas Hardy*. Catalog of Exhibit, Waterville, 1940.

DAICHES, DAVID. *The Novel in the Modern World*. Chicago: University of Chicago Press, 1960.

DUFFIN, H. C. *Thomas Hardy*. London: Longmans, Green, 1916.

FRIEDMAN, ALAN. *The Turn of the Novel*. Oxford: Oxford University Press, 1966.

GUERARD, ALBERT J. *Thomas Hardy*. New York: New Directions, 1964.

HARDY, EVELYN. *Thomas Hardy*. New York: St. Martin's Press, 1955.

HARDY, FLORENCE EMILY. *The Life of Thomas Hardy*. New York: St. Martin's Press, 1962.

JOHNSON, LIONEL. *The Art of Thomas Hardy*. New York: Haskell House, 1969.

KARL, FREDERICK. *A Reader's Guide to the Nineteenth Century British Novel*. New York: Farrar, Straus & Giroux, 1964.

SAXELBY, F. OUTWIN. *A Thomas Hardy Dictionary*. New York: Humanities Press, 1962.